WHAT I KNOW NOW

WHAT I KNOW NOW

Letters to My Younger Self

Edited by

E L L Y N S P R A G I N S

BROADWAY BOOKS
New York

Published in the United States by Broadway Books, an imprint
of The Doubleday Broadway Publishing Group, a division of
Random House, Inc., New York.

Visit our Web site at www.broadwaybooks.com

BROADWAY BOOKS and its logo, a letter B bisected on the
diagonal, are trademarks of Random House, Inc.

Book design by Michael Collica

Library of Congress Cataloging-in-Publication Data
What I know now : letters to my younger self / [edited by]
Ellyn Spragins.
p. cm.
1. Women—Psychology—Miscellanea. 2. Women—Conduct
of life—Miscellanea. 3. Women in public life—Biography.
4. Women in public life—Correspondence. 5. Celebrities—
Biography. 6. Celebrities—Correspondence. 7. Letters.
I. Spragins, Ellyn, 1947–

HQ1206.W58 2006
305.42—dc22
2005054216

ISBN-13: 978-0-7679-1789-6
ISBN-10: 0-7679-1789-8

PRINTED IN THE UNITED STATES OF AMERICA

20 19 18 17 16

For John Witty, whose
steadfast belief means everything

CONTENTS

ACKNOWLEDGMENTS

Among the many people who supported, inspired, and encouraged me as I wrote this book, I must first thank the women whose letters appear here. They were generous in making time for this project and courageous in being willing to expose their unglamorous moments. I salute them.

It would have been impossible to create *What I Know Now: Letters to My Younger Self* without the invisible machinery of my contributors' assistants, agents, and publicists, who patiently scheduled interviews, supplied photos, and followed up upon numerous details. I thank them all, particularly Jamie Smith, Ed Flathers, Bonnie Kramen, Jodi Reamer, Traecy Smith, Amber Williams, Sue Dorf, Kenton Edelin, Nicole Carey, Lee Gross, Kim Tinsley, Annie Whitworth, Trish Hughes, Fran Berry, and Heather McGinley.

I'm enormously grateful to Samantha Peitler, the steadiest, most resourceful assistant I could have asked for. Sam, thank you from the bottom of my heart.

New ideas are fragile things. I had the good luck to encounter Dawn Raffel, at *O, The Oprah Magazine,* who liked my idea well enough to publish the first letters in an article. My thoughtful, savvy agent, Debra Goldstein of the Creative Culture, embraced this project with wonderful enthusiasm and made me feel I could do anything. I'm glad you're in my corner, Debra. Kris Puopolo, already an editor of best-selling and award-winning authors at Doubleday Broadway, is a talent who will shape many more groundbreaking books. I feel lucky to have her as an editor. Beth Haymaker, also at Doubleday Broadway, weathered my cranky days with unfailing cheer.

Reaching out to the women in this book was possible because so many friends and acquaintances offered their assistance. I can't say how much this meant to me. I hope I can be as helpful to you someday, Susan and Tommy Thompson, Sara Nelson, Karen Oman, Barbara and Dennis Stern, David Whitford, Lynne Tapper, Joyce Roche, Rosemary and Larry Ward, Hank Gilman, Lindsay Scott, Mason Hoeller, Ed Gubman, Ann Price, Susie Bidel, Wendy Whitworth, Shelby Scarbrough, Nanci Morris, Bob and Robin Carey, John Sivright, Gaye Torrance, Ken Lehman, and Trish McEvoy.

The enterprising Sue Cooper conducted a key interview. I'm grateful for your persistence and speed, Sue.

To Chris Miles, my guru and champion from way back, bless you for a key piece of constructive criticism and for your big heart. My sincere thanks to Dan Goodgame, managing editor of *Fortune Small Business,* for kindly granting me a book leave at an inconvenient time. Thank you for your sharp eye, Ellen Cannon.

The March 12th Book Club is a rare group of perceptive and loyal friends, and their insights and high expectations sustained me. How lucky I am to be bound to Tricia Tunstall,

Emily Zacharias, Barbara Stern, Lisa Burrows, and Susan Thompson. My thanks to Dottie Serdenis, Ouidad Wise, and Janet Bamford, who listened to more details about this project than they could possibly have wanted to know. Thanks too, to Wally Konrad, Mary Clark, Rick Melcher, Katie Bliss, Sarah Bartlett, Josh Hyatt, and Karen McClean for their interest and support.

I'm blessed with a family that roots for me in every endeavor—especially this one. Betsy, John, Jodi, Brook, Chuck, Vania, Cricket, Thomas, and Cena—you guys are the best. I owe a special note of gratitude to my father, Pete Spragins, for his example of lifelong optimism and open-mindedness. My kids, Keenan and Tucker, helped give me the impetus to start this book and cheered me on when the going was rough. The steady confidence of my husband, John, helped keep my vision fresh and full of promise.

INTRODUCTION

If you could somehow postmark a letter back through time to your younger self, what age would you choose and what would the letter say? This is the question I asked dozens of extraordinary women. Some of the most creative, powerful, and famous women of our day were intrigued enough by this question to spend time with me as I helped each woman focus on the crucial moment in the past when she could have most used the understanding she now possesses. *What I Know Now: Letters to My Younger Self* contains their heartfelt responses to my question and shares wisdom that exceeded my greatest expectations.

I sought the insights of these remarkable women for a very simple reason. I miss my mother. She died in a plane crash when I was thirty-two. This was the first tragedy that ever befell my fortunate family and it seemed like an astonishing, theatrical mistake. Mom? Dead at sixty? On a plane headed to her great-aunt's funeral?

Before my father finished the sentence, "There were no

survivors," I sat up in bed, back perfectly erect, as if his voice contained an electrical current that had propelled me up and forward. In the same instant, I felt something else move forward. An invisible skein, so intricately threaded through my skeleton that I had never known it was there, seemed to rip itself out of my body and float away. I felt the departure of my mother first in my bones and sinews, which seemed hollow after that ethereal netting drifted off and dissolved in the dark Chicago night.

I know that my tragedy is a small one among the world's too-abundant supply of heartbreak. Indeed, in time I began to understand how richly indulged I was to have had a mother like mine for so long. She was loving, kind, loyal, with a large, lovely smile she wore often. Her name was Joyce.

But understanding that I was lucky didn't lessen the pain of her absence. As the years went by, I felt new grief as my own life gave me a context for hers. I lost my mother at thirty-two. She had lost hers at twenty-one. I had an ectopic pregnancy and lost a fallopian tube before adopting my daughter and getting pregnant with my son. She had suffered five miscarriages before having five children. As I navigated clumsily, painfully, and joyfully through life's passages, my appreciation for her and the way she conducted herself grew. But I felt a fresh, sharp stab of yearning each time she was not there to be my mother when I badly wanted mothering.

This book grew out of those moments. After the childish need for mothering passed, curiosity would remain. How had Mom handled this situation, overcome that obstacle, made peace with disappointments and betrayals? It wasn't just her advice that I wished for, though I think I would have welcomed it. I wanted to know what she thought and felt about key moments in her life—when they occurred and also what she would have thought today, when she could have used her life's wisdom to look back and reflect. What did she wish she had done, or wish she had not done? What would have seemed important to her now that seemed unimportant at the time? I wanted to see the underpinnings of her life—the joists, frame, and foundation, and how they were put together.

Then I realized that I didn't have to yearn for what was impossible. Every woman has struggles, regrets, "what ifs," and, as a result, wisdom to share. I could ask other women whom I respect and admire. That was the seed of this project, a gift to myself, and from an article in *O, The Oprah Magazine* in April 2003, it has grown. To my great pleasure, loving, kind, fascinating, famous, and accomplished women agreed to pull back the curtain on a part of their lives in order to contribute to this book. Now that it is complete, my hope is that *What I Know Now: Letters to My Younger Self* will help women better understand their own hurdles and, more importantly, that it will validate and honor their efforts to overcome them.

We don't always have the wisdom we require at the time we need it. We struggle. We worry. Often, only later do our choices make sense to us. What kind of advice would successful women like Senator Barbara Boxer, actress Olympia Dukakis, or activist Heather Mills McCartney give to their younger selves?

The answers are in your hands, in the form of letters back in time—and they may surprise you. As I helped the contributors plan their missives, I noticed that, as a rule, they had no difficulty coming up with a message to convey. More often, my task was to help them pick which challenging moment in their lives to focus on, out of so many.

These interviews were strikingly different from most of the ones I've conducted during nearly twenty-five years as a journalist. They were personal, of course, but that only begins to explain their emotional texture. I was asking terribly smart, talented women with enormous demands on their time to pause and reflect upon hidden aspects of their lives—their mistakes, vulnerabilities, or fears. The conversation would often lead to one anecdote after another as we teased out the knot of circumstances wrapped around a dark moment in a woman's life. That's revealing a lot to a perfect stranger. But they did so with candor and generosity, and I am honored by their trust.

Though their advice, and the age group at which it's aimed, varies widely, you may notice some common elements. Each of the contributors feels real kindness for the girl, young adult, or middle-aged woman she once was. There are remarkably few messages that are strategic or action-oriented, such as "Quit that job" or "Move to Montana." Instead, for most women the essential information they wanted to convey had to do with how to navigate intense emotions. For them, the battle wasn't on the outside; it was on the inside. I think of *Today*'s Ann Curry worrying that her true self was being erased in her first job, or Olympic gymnast Shannon Miller feeling that the world expected an eye-popping encore after she retired from competition.

In many cases, it's possible to see a connection between a woman's ostensible weakness, revealed in her letter, and a current strength in her life or work. After being burdened with free-floating phobias and foibles as a child, cartoonist Roz Chast now makes her living by turning fear and foibles into pictures we can laugh at. Having suffered in an oppressive relationship rather than be alone with herself, Eileen Fisher now makes clothing for women who are, above all else, centered and at ease with themselves.

Only in hindsight can we see that our fears and worries were unwarranted, that insecurities and doubts were just illusions, or that we should have taken a risk or dared something new sooner. It's humbling to compare yourself to the women in this book. But at the same time, it's encouraging to know that even women at the top of their fields have suffered private fears, longings, and missteps. To know that these talented women didn't enter the world as finished products—confident, successful, glamorous—is to understand that it's within our grasp to reach loftier levels than we might have dreamed of.

Choosing to grow during trying life passages can be lonely work. I hope this book will make that choice less solitary because you'll be in the company of great women.

"You've got the guts to find your own purpose."

I T'S ODD TO think of a former secretary of state as someone who worries about fitting in, but for a long time
Madeleine Albright did. In a group, she paid attention rather
than interrupt. Sitting in her roomy office at the Albright
Group, in Washington, D.C., Madeleine recalled her need to
be liked and accepted with no regrets. "In the end I don't
think it was a disadvantage. Wanting and needing to be liked
is part of what got me to where I am."

Wearing a red suit and brown leather Lucchese cowboy
boots when I met her, Madeleine, sixty-nine, seduced me
with her forthright, unpretentious manner. She treated me as
an equal, even though I've never owned cowboy boots or a
cabinet title. Smaller than I expected, she held her body very
still during our meeting. Her blue eyes seemed to swallow my
words with a gravity that lingered even when she laughed.
Don't forget this is a woman who has spent numberless hours
with world leaders, including Pope John Paul II, the Dalai

Lama, Nelson Mandela, and grappled with genocide, war, U.S. embassy bombings, and U.S. cruise missile attacks on suspected terrorist camps in Afghanistan, among other crises.

Born Marie Jana Korbel in Prague, Madeleine and her family emigrated to the United States when she was a child. Apple-cheeked and round in high school, as she describes herself, Madeleine worked hard to seem casual and American. Her efforts were often undone by a serious streak that revealed itself through bossy outbursts, such as when she turned in a fellow student for talking during study hall. After attending Kent, a private girls' school in Denver, Madeleine went to Wellesley College on scholarship and married journalist Joe Albright three days after graduating.

Her letter is addressed to herself in the spring of 1982, at age forty-four, when she was still reeling from the breakdown of her marriage of twenty-three years. Shortly after Joe announced that he wanted a divorce, she accepted an offer to join the faculty at Georgetown University School of Foreign Service. At that time in her life she had already earned a master of arts and a Ph.D. from Columbia University, acted as chief legislative assistant to Senator Edmund Muskie, and worked on the National Security Council's staff. In her new position, she was charged with creating a program that would encourage women to enter international relations, and she was expected to serve as a role model for those young women.

Dear Madeleine,

You will get through this fog and uncertainty—and you'll do it in the best possible way. You won't become cynical, stoical, or hard-bitten over the loss you're feeling. Over the next ten years you'll rebuild and reinvent yourself, finding success—and tremendous satisfaction.

The truth is, you've got the guts to find your own purpose and the integrity to fulfill it on your own terms. Your parents taught you to strive to achieve all you can, with the gifts that you have. Now you're about to direct those gifts toward finding your voice and using it to serve your country in ways that will surprise you.

When your students ask you how you have managed to be married and have children and work at the same time, you feel like a phony because you think you haven't succeeded at that. It's hard to feel qualified as a role model. But you are.

It will take years before you realize that you already are a good role model. But ultimately you'll inspire far more women than you'd ever predict. Twenty-three years from now when women say that they're choosing a career in international relations, the thing you'll enjoy most is telling them that there is no formula, that everybody must choose their own path.

With confidence,
Madeleine

MAYA ANGELOU

Poet, Author, Playwright

"Don't let anybody raise you. You've been raised."

BORN MARGUERITE JOHNSON, Dr. Maya Angelou was raised by her mother, Lady Vivian Baxter, a self-possessed, successful entrepreneur and businesswoman who owned a hotel and wore diamonds in her ears. Unmarried, Marguerite was pregnant when she finished high school in the summer of 1945. Her son was born in September and she decided to leave home two months later.

Leaving the comfort of her mother's big house, which had live-in help, was characteristic of Dr. Angelou's courage and fierce sense of independence. She has gone on to embrace—and excel at—a dizzying array of disciplines. She speaks French, Italian, Spanish, and West African Fanti. She has danced onstage, composed music, written plays, directed and acted in movies. In the 1960s, Dr. Martin Luther King, Jr., asked her to become the northern coordinator for the Southern Christian Leadership Conference, and in 1993, President-elect Bill Clinton requested that she write a poem for his inauguration.

Dr. Angelou has written prodigiously: six autobiographies, including the best-selling *I Know Why the Caged Bird Sings*, published by Random House in 1969; three children's books; six plays and two screenplays; numerous books of poetry and other books. *Just Give Me a Cool Drink of Water 'fore I Diiie*, a collection of her poetry, earned a Pulitzer Prize nomination in 1971. In 1981, she was appointed to a lifetime post as Reynolds Professor of American Studies at Wake Forest University.

This avalanche of achievement could not have seemed more improbable on the day the seventeen-year-old Marguerite left her mother's house with a two-month-old son in her arms. She had found a job, a room with cooking privileges down the hall, and a landlady who would baby-sit. Here is what Dr. Angelou, seventy-eight, would say to her younger self.

Dear Marguerite,

You're itching to be on your own. You don't want anybody telling you what time you have to be in at night or how to raise your baby. You're going to leave your mother's big comfortable house and she won't stop you, because she knows you too well.

But listen to what she says:

When you walk out of my door, don't let anybody raise you—you've been raised.

You know right from wrong.

In every relationship you make, you'll have to show readiness to adjust and make adaptations.

Remember, you can always come home.

You will go home again when the world knocks you down—or when you fall down in full view of the world. But only for two or three weeks at a time. Your mother will pamper you and feed you your favorite meal of red beans and rice. You'll make a practice of going home so she can liberate you again—one of the greatest gifts, along with nurturing your courage, that she will give you.

Be courageous, but not foolhardy.

Walk proud as you are,
Maya

RACHEL ASHWELL

Creator of Shabby Chic

∼⊙∼

"Don't leave school just yet."

DEEP PILLOWS AND feather beds are at hand. Plump armchairs wear slouchy white denim or cream linen slipcovers. Worn tables bear honorable scars and nicks. In the unpretentious slipcover and flea market world of Rachel Ashwell, coziness counts more than pedigree. A self-taught designer and entrepreneur who grew up in Britain, Rachel, forty-six, says her biggest fear is mediocrity. To her, an ordinary decor looks familiar—because it's been done before. "Mediocrity is a superficial effort—what happens when a project is done without passion," she says. Her company, Rachel Ashwell Shabby Chic, based in Los Angeles, celebrates plain design and refurnished furniture, edited by a strict "Less is more" principle. "I can't bear cluttered closets. A cluttered cupboard is a cluttered mind," she says.

The concept has lured customers around the world, including celebrities like Britney Spears and Pamela Anderson. Her fifteen-year-old company, with more than $10 million in revenues and 125 employees, is expanding quickly. In addition to six stores, five books, and a TV show associated with the company, Rachel Ashwell Shabby Chic spread in 2004 to department stores like Bloomingdale's (with a new line of sleepwear) and Target stores (with bedding, furniture, rugs, and other products for the kitchen, living room, and elsewhere).

Despite her successful track record, until recently Rachel was uncomfortable if someone she didn't know approached her at a party. She explains why in her letter, written to herself at age sixteen, when she dropped out of school. "In America people think of everybody in Britain as Cambridge- or Oxford-educated and madly intellectual, but they're not," she says.

After dropping out, she found employment as an au pair in Britain and moved in with the family she worked for. A few months later, she relocated into a room in a Council Flats building, which was government-subsidized and "pretty Dickensian," she says. Rachel's working-class floor mates included quite a few drunks. Every tenant shared a hall bathroom. You had to put change into a meter for hot water.

In time, of course, she became an expert at replacing hard edges and dark gloom with soft cushions and pastel colors. That feat is detailed in *The Shabby Chic Home,* an account of Rachel's unglitzy renovation of her beloved Malibu home, which she later sold. Her special alchemy lies in the way she allows a room to answer to a primal need, described by poet Maya Angelou: "The ache for home lives in all of us, the safe place where we can go as we are and not be questioned."

⟋⟋⟋

Dear Rachel,

Don't leave school just yet. You're sixteen, eager to get a job and get on with it. This willingness to move on—no, actually it's like a compulsion, isn't it?—will serve you well. What would you say if I told you that your love for design and decorating, combined with that incredible drive to start the next thing, will lead to a business with your name on it that generates more than $10 million in annual sales?

So, being impatient will be an asset. But you need school, too— not because you need book knowledge but because you should have more experience with learning. Without that, you'll struggle. Even in your mid-forties, when you're doing something silly, like reading instructions for a new appliance or reading People magazine, you'll have to keep bringing yourself back to focus. You'll love what you do. Your life will be like a big box of candy every day. But the problem will be savoring the one in your mouth. You'll no sooner bite into one piece than you'll have your eye on the Milky Way over there.

Many entrepreneurs and artists skip the traditional educational path. Still, one thing that's really wonderful is that if you follow certain rhythms in life, the tracks that most people pursue, things do tend to work out. Without that evolution of character building, though, it's hard to catch up. At forty-six, I think I'm just beginning to catch up. I've always been quite nervous about crowds and parties. I worry because I don't trust strangers. I just didn't allow myself to go with that rhythm when it was the right time to connect with people, so you should. I didn't cultivate friendships or a sense of myself, which is why you must.

Now that I have a daughter who's older than you are, I understand that the experience of being around other kids is as important a part of education as classroom material. I see all these dramas she and her friends have. They hate one another; then they love one another. It's just what they do. Without the bumps and bruises of a school's social scene, you're going to be defenseless when conflicts arise. You'll be so uncomfortable around confrontation, for example, that there will be many instances in your future life where you'll walk away without presenting your point of view.

Impatience and restlessness will lead you to one decision in particular that you'll regret. After establishing a career based on making houses into cozy sanctuaries, you'll sell the first house you ever bought, in Malibu. You'll think it's important to have more communal space, something bigger. You won't take into consideration the importance of the place where you made your family's memories. That's what comes of not having the intellectual habit of thinking things through and making a decision for the right reason. Life will be your school, and you'll be successful. But with a mentor and some training, your success could be really amazing.

With patience,
Rachel

BARBARA BOXER

U.S. Senator from California

"Don't be so quick to dismiss another human being."

AFTER SHORT CAREERS as a stockbroker and a journal-ist, Barbara Boxer, now sixty-five, found her voice as an advocate in politics. It was like a race car at full throttle suddenly finding traction. Barely five feet tall, Boxer, a passionate champion of the environment, childhood education, and women's rights, sometimes has to stand on a box to see over the podium at press conferences. In recent years, the Brooklyn-born Democrat has become better known for criticizing key Republican moves. She fiercely censured the war in Iraq. She signed a House member's complaint about Ohio voting problems during the 2004 presidential election, which forced Congress to debate the snafu before certifying President Bush's victory. Her vehement opposition to Condoleezza Rice's nomination as secretary of state inspired a skit on *Saturday Night Live*.

Far from scaring voters away, Barbara's boldness seems to have endeared her to Californians. Running for her third term in 2004, she received more than 6.9 million votes, the highest number ever tallied for any Senate candidate, beating opponent Bill Jones by twenty percentage points. There's also talk of a Boxer for President campaign on Internet blogs, but she says she has no interest in running.

Though her success looks effortless, she had to learn that passion, clarity, and determination are not enough to ensure victory. The first time she ran for office—a spot on the Marin County Board of Supervisors—she lost. "One of my biggest faults when I started out in politics was being judgmental. At that young age, I didn't really have the patience to hear why someone might have a different point of view from mine," she said. Four years later, in 1976, she ran again and won. This letter is for the thirty-two-year-old Boxer, mother of a seven-year-old boy and a five-year-old girl, as she was preparing to run for office for the first time.

◦◦◦

Dear Barbara,

You're full of fire. You're passionate about quality education, safe streets, the environment—all of these things. I know you feel these things in your heart and you feel them strongly, but look, you have to understand that the next person may hold their beliefs with the same amount of passion that you have. Don't be so judgmental about other people. Don't be so quick to dismiss another human being. Don't jump to the conclusion that another person just doesn't get it or isn't wise enough just because he doesn't agree with you.

The name of the game in politics is to move forward an issue you deeply believe in. You're just starting out and young enough to be impatient when people don't see your point of view. Stop and listen to what you're saying: I can't believe you feel that way! *And:* How could you possibly think that way? *You've shut off the potential to learn from that person you're talking to and you'll be less of a person for it. In the end, you'll lose what matters most—the chance to advance an issue you care about.*

There's something else you may not want to face: It's easier to be judgmental. It's less work to see everything in black and white. But every single person is as important as you are and has a story to tell, just like you do. Open up your mind to other points of view—and you may not have to experience how losing an election can take you down a peg or two.

Your staunchest supporter,
Senator Boxer

$\sim\!\!\mathcal{Q}\!\!\sim$

"Flex that muscle in your heart."

BEING THE DAUGHTER of Warren Buffett, chairman of Berkshire Hathaway, legendary investor and billionaire, has been easy, says Susie Buffett, fifty-two, his oldest child. But not for the reason you may think. "I didn't grow up with all this money," she says. "My parents didn't come from families with money, and when I was really young, we had no money, so I didn't grow up entitled." The ease comes from the close relationship she has enjoyed with both parents. As a toddler, she often felt the need to escape from Howie, her tornado of a brother, whose energy was overwhelming. "My Dad would come in from work and it felt like he was rescuing me. He would sing to me and rock me to sleep every night," she remembers. "He and I have been attached in a way that is very nice."

That connection has been the source of special comfort since Susie's mother, Susan Thompson Buffett, died of a stroke on the day before her daughter's birthday in 2004, after battling oral cancer. Susie got a big box of presents from her mother the next day, which she had not yet opened a year later when we talked by phone. During that year, she had moved her office up to the same floor as her father's in their Omaha, Nebraska, office building and assumed the chairmanship of the Susan Thompson Buffett Foundation, formerly the Buffett Foundation. She is also the chairman of the Susan A. Buffett Foundation, which aims to change the face of early childhood education for low-income children through Educare of Omaha.

Her mother's warmth and demonstrativeness were coupled with a decisive bias toward action. Long before the family had foundations and the net worth to fund them, Susie's mom began correcting social ills wherever she encountered them. When Susie was fifteen, her mother asked her father to mortgage the house in order to raise bail money for an African-American boy she believed was innocent of the rape charge he had been arrested for. Warren agreed to it. The boy was tried and found not guilty. What did Omaha think of such behavior? Susie's mom didn't care. She hung a poster in the family room that read PROTEST AGAINST THE RISING TIDE OF CONFORMITY.

With such a strong role model, Susie, who bears a remarkable resemblance to her mother, naturally gravitated toward activism and volunteer work. After stints working for Century 21, *The New Republic,* and *U.S. News & World Report,* Susie and her husband moved to Omaha, where she has been a volunteer and board member for many local organizations and has raised her two children. Among these organizations are Girls Incorporated and a children's theater that functions in part as a social service agency. She also serves on the national boards of Girls Incorporated, the Ounce of Prevention Fund, and DATA (Debt, AIDS, Trade, Africa). Susie and her mother, both longtime fans of Bono and U2, visited Bono's house in France during her mother's last summer. Bono's music, says Susie, helped her mother through a lot of her illness. "She used to fall asleep listening to 'All I Want Is You,'" remembers Susie, who stayed with her during months of her hospitalizations and recovery.

Amid her grief, she feels an enormous sense of gratitude, which inspired this letter to herself at seventeen.

Dear Sooz,

You are so blessed. By accident of birth, you landed in a home with two spectacular parents. You already know that, at some level. You're not the typical teenager who can't stand her parents. Your house is the one where everyone hangs out—your dad calls it "the YMCA."

Still, you won't begin to appreciate the true scope of your parents' gifts to you for years. That's only natural. But I want to alert you to one of them, so you can recognize its value early. It's been so ever present in your life that it would be easy to take for granted: your mother's capacity for unconditional love and acceptance. She could find something good to say about Charles Manson.

This kind of acceptance doesn't spring up spontaneously. It arises from an ability—a genius, really, in your mom's case—to empathize deeply with other people. Does it come from all that time she spent alone as a child with rheumatic fever? She had to be inside herself a lot, perhaps reflecting on matters that would escape most healthy children's notice. Whatever the reason, her empathetic knack is what is behind some of her unconventional behavior.

Remember when she used to pack you and your brothers into the car and visit the Omaha housing projects? The police used to stop her because she was the only white lady in that area, and warn her that she could get kidnapped. She paid them no mind. And think about how she is with your friends, Susie. Is there another mother you know who is willing to talk about sex and procure birth control for teenagers? The 1960s will come to be known as the period that shook up the country's assumptions about blacks, sex, and countless other issues. It hasn't happened yet, though. Because of her talent for identifying with someone else's problem, your mom is way ahead of the rest of the country. Empathy has led her to become extraordinarily accepting of others, but it's also what makes her comfortable with acting unconventionally.

So, Susie, flex that muscle in your heart. The bigger you can make it, the more you will develop the empathy your mother has. It's one of the best ways you'll be able to honor her after she's gone. Empathy doesn't have to lead you to the routes she will follow, which may be a temptation, given your resemblance to her. The important thing is that it becomes your compass, too.

With love,
Susie

ROZ CHAST

Cartoonist

─◦◦◦─

"Being an adult is better than being a kid."

THE WOMEN IN Roz Chast's world flirt daringly with leaving soccer momhood, fantasize about a remote control with buttons labeled "Brush your teeth" and "Change that awful shirt," and are likely to receive a "Bad Mom" card for serving orange soda to their children when they run out of juice. Populated with frumpy, gawky, and braces-bedecked family members, Roz's cartoons put our secret obsessions and private worries on center stage.

The mother of two teenagers, Ian and Nina, Roz lives in Connecticut with her husband, humor writer Bill Franzen. She has drawn thousands of cartoons, mostly for *The New Yorker* since she became a regular contributor in 1978. Two collections are gathered in *The Party, After You Left: Collected Cartoons 1995–2003* and *Childproof: Cartoons*. Roz's befuddled characters may soon join Bart Simpson and Family Guy on television. In November of 2004, Roz signed a development deal to create a short family-oriented comedy pilot for the ABC Family television network.

Roz's talent for identifying graceless moments and every-day neuroses grew out of her experience as a young hypo-chondriac living in Brooklyn with her parents, a high school teacher and assistant principal. "They were worriers, too. We were just peas in a pod. Worried peas in a worried pod," says Roz. Her mother regularly consulted a blue *Merck Manual,* which lists thousands of descriptions of diseases and medical conditions. The impressionable young Roz found ample rea-son to fret whenever she dipped into this tome. Here she writes to herself at nine years old.

Roz,

   You are not going to get leprosy. I promise.

   Or lockjaw.

   Again, I promise. Don't ask me how I know. I just do.

   Those nights you lie in bed feeling that your tongue is suddenly eight times bigger than normal, testing your jaw for stiffness, gulping down saliva repeatedly to gauge if you're having difficulty swallowing—they're over. YOU WILL NOT GET SICK.

   I'm not one of those adults who think kids have the best lives. I know how much the world's traps and dangers burden you. Ever since you learned that Helen Keller sensed the heat of an electrical fire by putting her hands against the wall, you occupy your idle minutes fretting about the wires behind the plaster. Ever since you read how Trixie Belden had to suck the venom out of her brother's foot, you've been keeping a watchful eye out for rattlesnakes on the occasions when you're forced to leave the safety of your family's Brooklyn apartment.

But you're going to be okay. Roz, here's the other thing I want you to know: Being an adult is better than being a kid. You're going to grow up—healthy and whole—and everything you're feeling now is going to be great material for your work.

From Somebody Who Knows

∽◌◌◡◡∼

"Try more things. Cross some lines."

I T ' S   A   S I M P L E   thing, but swimming has played a charged
role in Breena Clarke's life. In her novel, *River, Cross My
Heart,* her protagonist, twelve-year-old Johnnie Mae, swims
in the Potomac to expel her grief over her sister's death—and
to claim a place for herself at the new community pool, in
which black children aren't allowed.

Breena's mother was one source of inspiration for Johnnie
Mae. Her mother loved to swim. But as a child, she was allowed only to gaze at a nearby pool from the outside as the heat
bounced off her head. Breena was struck by the intensity with
which her mother still felt this injustice some fifty or sixty years
later, and so she wove Johnnie Mae's story around it.

She wrote her book, which was an Oprah Book Club se-
lection in 1999, on the strength of her imagination—having
never learned to swim herself. Finally, in her late forties, she
did, and she says it has changed her life. "I realize I have a
strong body that can accomplish things. I bought a bicycle. All

those years I could have had more fun doing things like this," she says.

Breena was raised by parents who believed that appearance, public deportment, and education were paramount for well-mannered middle-class colored girls. Much of the message was encoded in a torturous hair-straightening ritual that she and her sister, Cheryl, endured until they went away to college. "We were battling racial stereotypes through our hair," recalls Breena. "We had been bombarded with the idea that our hair in its natural state was not good."

By the time she went to Webster College in 1969, turbulent antiwar and black power ideologies were sweeping college campuses. After her mother dropped her off at college, Clarke stepped into the shower and emerged with her first Afro, an official revolutionary. Her letter is to that young woman.

⁓◦⁓

Honey,

Your hair is not politics. It is not about the war. It does not make you Angela Davis or Sonia Sanchez or Diana Sands. The Afro is only a hairstyle. A whole lot of people are making the same mistake you are—wearing Afros and dashikis and thinking they're life issues. Brainy as you are, you don't know that hair is just hair.

I tell you this because right now you are drawing invisible boundaries for yourself everywhere. You're creating a set of beliefs about yourself that are going to box you in. For example, now that you're wearing an Afro, you think you've crossed the Rubicon. Your hair will have to be nappy until the day you die. Your brain is telling you that you can't be crossing the line.

There are other barriers you're erecting. You're spending a lot of energy getting out of your phys ed classes because you're either a sports type of person or you're a Shakespeare type of person and you can't be crossing the line.

Breena, you are cheating yourself. You are guaranteeing yourself a sedentary life. Worse, you won't know how strong and athletic your body is. You won't get to enjoy using it until you're forty-nine years old. That's too long to wait.

You may never get to send your soul into a song the way you secretly want to. Some people think that deep inside of you there is a singer, but you believe that you are not. The truth is, you've never allowed yourself to find out what kind of voice you have because you can't be crossing the line.

Breena, honey, try more things. Cross some lines. Learning to swim won't stop you from reading Shakespeare. Finding your voice won't stop you from writing novels. You should be cooking on all four burners.

Love,
Breena

~⟨℮⟩~

"It's time to be bold about who you really are."

THOUGH YOU WOULDN'T know it from watching her on NBC's *Today,* Ann Curry has a way of throwing her whole body into a conversation. She settles her long limbs into a chair, leans forward, and listens deeply, all parts on alert. The calm, mellifluous voice that reports daily on wars, floods, and famine in Ann's role as news anchor has a magnetic effect in a confidential chat.

She's the kind of person who might have inspired author George Eliot when she wrote, "Oh, the comfort, the inexpressible comfort of feeling safe with a person; having neither to weigh thoughts nor to measure words but to pour them all out, just as it is, chaff and grain together, knowing that a faithful hand will take and sift them, keeping what is worth keeping, and then, with the breath of kindness, blow the rest away."

If Ann, now forty-seven, emanates acceptance, it's due in part to the experience of dislocation that she writes about in this letter to herself at age twenty-two. By the standards of today's diverse racial combinations, her lovely face seems only slightly exotic, but as a kid she was made to feel that her mixed-race look was radically different. "My entire life people have looked at me and interpreted what they would from seeing that I am unusual-looking. When I gave birth to my son and he was blond and blue-eyed, people thought I was the nanny. I swear to you. I actually was asked just two months ago if I was a baby-sitter at my daughter's school," she says.

The winner of two Emmy awards as a reporter for KCBS in Los Angeles and four Golden Mike awards, Ann put herself through the University of Oregon School of Journalism. She graduated in 1978, the same year that her father, Bob Curry, finished college—the first two members of the family to do so. "My best friend was always my father. He would tell me I could do anything. For all the issues and insecurities and suffering and pain of trying to figure things out at this age, there was a person who was fervent in his belief in me," says Ann.

◦◦◦

Hey there, Anner,

I'm watching you fend for yourself at your first job in a six-man newsroom in Medford, Oregon, population fifty thousand. Every day that you walk into that smoke-filled all-male stronghold, you feel like it could be your last day on the job. You're doing twice as many stories as your middle-aged colleagues, but failure seems to lurk just around the corner. One of these gentlemen even said it to your face: "You have no news judgment—and besides, you can't carry the camera."

Oh yeah? Watch me, you thought, ever more ferocious in your determination. You feel energized knowing that your performance could pave the way—or close the door—for the women behind you. But there's a profound fear underneath the bravado. Will you—the half-Japanese outsider who never fit in while growing up in all-white Ashland, Oregon—have to change some deep part of yourself to make it in this world? Your heart is weighed down by the worry that you'll never be seen for who you really are, that you'll always be misunderstood.

The irony is that you, Ann, have struggled your whole life against being put in an easily categorized box. And now, the girl whose appearance always prompted questions like "What are you? Hispanic? Asian?" is thrusting herself into an industry where looks count for so much. The girl who's happy in grungy flannel shirts and jeans has to learn how to pluck her eyebrows, put on makeup, and wear suits. You're conforming to what people expect you to look like—but it's scaring the heck out of you.

Think back. You've never bent to those kind of expectations before. Remember that your Japanese immigrant mother wanted so much for you to be pretty and popular that when you were in fifth grade, she hemmed your skirts to miniskirt length and bought you a pair of go-go boots. You wore the mini to school and ripped out the hem because you knew it didn't matter if you were pretty or fit in. You wanted to be smart.

You were happy being a maverick. You were extremely opinionated, but you were also extremely nonjudgmental. No matter what anybody thought, if they truly felt it, it was okay with you. You refused to judge other people.

But now you're in the real world and the real world seems to have no hesitation about judging you on appearance, so you're changing as fast as you can. You've cut off your waist-length hair, gotten a perm, and you wear floppy bow ties to the station. You're even cussing. No more "Horsefeathers!" or "Heavens to Mergatroid!" You're spewing real curse words to make sure these old guys don't feel threatened by having a woman in the newsroom. Is it surprising that you hardly recognize yourself?

You should understand that being different is fantastic. In fact, rejoice in all those things that make you different. Ultimately, it's not how you look or what group you're in that will determine your success in the world. I think you can carve new territory, you can do something completely out of the box, and if it is an act of love and goodness, it will be completely embraced—as bizarre as that may seem.

If you can have faith in your real self, you'll suffer less. You won't waste valuable time that could be spent on more important things. At forty-seven, I sometimes feel like a late bloomer. I feel it would have been possible to do much more, much sooner, if I hadn't been so worried. What I know now after the loss of my mother, my brother, and all the suffering I've covered as a news reporter is that there's no time to waste. It's time to be bold about who you really are.

With love,
Ann

CAROLYN   DEAVER

Breast Cancer Survivor

"Don't let your emotional needs go begging."

"YOU'RE JUST OFF, not quite moored. You've lost your footing." This is how Carolyn Deaver, sixty-seven, describes what it was like to be told she had cancer at the age of fifty. All her reference points were gone. She was in her own skin, but it felt suddenly foreign.

Carolyn, whose husband, Mike, was deputy chief of staff for President Reagan, had just accepted a job at the Children's National Medical Center to head up the organization's fund-raising when she got the news in 1989. She was so completely upended that she planned to tell her new boss to find someone else to fill the position. Fortunately, a social worker advised her to request a month's delay before starting and a modified work plan that would allow her to take Fridays off for chemotherapy, giving her the weekend to recover.

That advice was one of the few useful points of guidance she received. Another support she stumbled on when it was a pilot program is called Look Good . . . Feel Better (LGFB). LGFB offers beauty strategies to counter the appearance-related side effects of chemotherapy and radiation upon women with cancer. "I think one of the things that you try to do when you have cancer is to try not to look the part. You become the object of pity, or too much sympathy, maybe. So anything you can do to feel good about yourself and present yourself with confidence keeps that away," she explains.

Having teenagers in the house was another complication. Once she lost her hair from chemotherapy, Carolyn was in the habit of shedding her wig after she came home from work or another public venue. Her son, Blair, ignited a small tempest when he asked his mother if she could keep her wig on at home. "His sister, Amanda, let him have it," remembers Carolyn. "She said, 'It may make you feel better, but you're not even thinking about how she feels.'"

The breast cancer experience led Carolyn to a job heading LGFB, as vice president of the CTFA Foundation, a Washington, D.C., organization which funds the program. Over the last twelve years, LGFB has served 400,000 women in the United States. During nearly fifteen years there, Carolyn expanded the program to men and teenagers and fostered its growth internationally in fourteen countries. After another recent experience with cancer, this time in her uterus, she had a hysterectomy and decided to retire from LGFB in order to travel, hike, and get involved with some charitable organizations.

Her first cancer experience changed her point of view about how to live. She says she learned that one should do the following: "Treat yourself. Indulge yourself. Put yourself first. It's a hard thing to try to do, especially for mothers. It was not an instant change for me." In her letter, Carolyn, who underwent a mastectomy and chemotherapy, offers some key thoughts to herself just after her diagnosis.

⟋⟍

Dear Carolyn,

I know you are reeling with the news—you've just learned that you have breast cancer. I also know you want to scream at the next person who says to you, "I know how you feel!" Even your husband said it, and he had his head taken off. How could they know the anger you are feeling? Why me, when I took good care of myself? *How could they know about the anger stirred up when good-intentioned friends suggest that your cancer was caused by stress? We all seek to reduce the stress in our lives, but we can't be hermits and wall ourselves off from conflicts and cares.*

What you need to remember is that anger in any form will only make things worse and will limit your ability to cope with the concept of having cancer and the reality of treatment. Anger will also limit your ability to get better, and that is where your focus should be—on getting better.

It won't be easy, because you're already dealing with some extremely stressful circumstances. Your husband is grappling with an addiction. You've got a fifteen-year-old son and a twenty-year-old daughter who need your attention. And you're about to start a new job, which you don't see that you can possibly do now.

Please, go join a support group, even though you're afraid that if you do, someone in the group will die. Or find a therapist who's familiar with cancer. You have a month to make up your mind whether to get a lumpectomy or a mastectomy. While you will plunge into gathering information on the medical side of cancer, don't let your emotional needs go begging. Sometimes you can't explore the thoughts and fears and ideas on your own.

And most importantly, instead of being a "Why me?" victim, think of yourself as a cancer survivor—every minute, every day, and every year. It may sound a bit heroic, but then that's what you are: your very own heroine.

Live well . . .
Carolyn

OLYMPIA DUKAKIS

Actress

❧

"Learn how to celebrate."

O LYMPIA DUKAKIS OOZES integrity—not a quality that often comes to mind when describing an actress. Her strength of character stems from an early, long-lasting resistance to the designations pinned on her. As a daughter of Greek immigrant parents, she was expected to be obedient and submissive. Headstrong and willful, she rebelled against the "good Greek daughter" label, causing years of conflict with her mother. She grew up on the streets of a tough neighborhood in Lowell, Massachusetts. There she fought against ethnic slurs in regular clashes with Irish, French, Syrian, and Armenian kids. At age eleven, she carried a knife.

Her objective, she writes in *Ask Me Again Tomorrow: A Life in Progress,* was "to define *myself,* not fall into the role others wanted to define for me. I'd done it from as early as I can remember; first with my parents, then as a schoolgirl, later as an actress and wife and mother." The quest, which she says is ongoing at age seventy-two, scrapes away her comfort zone.

"I know who I am," Olympia intoned as Rose Castorini, the resolute Italian matriarch in *Moonstruck,* for which she received an Academy Award for Best Supporting Actress, the New York Film Critics Award, the Los Angeles Film Critics Award, and the Golden Globe Award. But she reports that she doesn't feel such certainty. Another line, from Martin Sherman's one-woman show, *Rose,* resonates more deeply: "Maybe there's a joy in not belonging."

Speaking with me by phone, Olympia, with a throaty laugh, confesses that her seventh decade hasn't brought the serenity so many people imagine will grace their later years. "I used to have the feeling that as I got older, life would be more peaceful—that's what many older people say. I'm not one of those people. I look back and there are many things I regret," she admits.

She discusses some of them in her letter, written to herself in her late forties, after her husband, Louie Zorich, experienced a brutal car crash in 1977. The accident fractured and dislocated his hip and shattered his knee. He endured three months of hospitalization, followed by years of painful physical therapy and hip- and knee-replacement surgeries. The night that Louie came home, after he was installed in a hospital bed in the first-floor dining room of their Georgian Colonial in Montclair, New Jersey, Olympia wept at the kitchen table. The doctors said he would walk only with canes or crutches. They had three children, Christina, Peter, and Stefan, under the age of thirteen. With Louie, whom she sometimes calls Lulubelle, unable to work, Olympia became the family's breadwinner. Running the Whole Theater (her consuming but poor-paying passion) would have to be squeezed in at the margins while pursuing more lucrative work. "In those years I never stopped," she remembers.

Dear Oly,

A fine mess you've gotten yourself into this time.

You wake up worried about money almost every day. Your kitchen functions like a war room. Charts and timetables cover the wall so that you can plot your ever-changing schedule at the theater and in Manhattan, where you chase paying jobs, against the kids' after-school activities. When you spot a precious square inch of blank space—your free time—you dedicate it to watching one of the kids' games. The school has been sending letters to you, stressing the importance of your support. What with your charts, the kids' bikes, and your brother and sister-in-law's aid, everybody seems to be landing where they're supposed to, more or less on time.

You're not really dealing with feelings, though—yours or the kids'. You're so taken up with just surviving that you're ignoring the most important issue: The kids have effectively lost their father. Louie is fully absorbed with putting his body back together. You need to talk to Christina, Peter, and Stefan about that and what it means to all of you. And you should understand that, in a way, the kids are losing you, too. You're so busy that you're absent. It's not an overstatement to say that they feel like their family is crumbling.

Unless you change what you're doing, the kids will have to confront these issues later in life. And you'll wake up in middle of the night and wonder why you didn't do some of these things differently. I hesitate to say all this because you labor so relentlessly and you're trying so hard. But you need to learn how to celebrate— not just to suffer. It sounds impossible, doesn't it? How, in the midst of all this turmoil, can you possibly find a way to feel good about what's happening?

One way is to realize that being strong doesn't require that you deny yourself pleasures. You don't have to "earn" them by toiling harder than every other workhorse. You're unnaturally good at deferring gratification, Olympia. Learn that you can be responsible for your children and enjoy them at the same time. Talk to them about what's happening and, even more important, listen to what they say.

What could also ease your stress is a different way of thinking about how we travel through this world. There's no ladder to success. The rhythm of life runs in cycles. There are times in the darkness and times in the light. The energy of life is like the rain forest in Borneo. Things live, grow, die, fall to the forest floor, rot, and then they are born again. Remember what Mother says? Everyone gets kicked down the stairs. This is one of those times.

You must embrace these changes. As difficult as they are, they will pass. But you mustn't bury or deny the darkness. You gotta live through it; you can't cheat.

Even now, you have a lot to look forward to. Birthdays, for example. You and Louie have rarely made merry on those days. Sometimes you've forgotten them altogether. But that will change. You'll understand that purposefully capturing happy moments expands your soul. On your fortieth wedding anniversary, you'll have an enormous party at your New York City loft with fifty people raising their glasses to you. In time you'll start to rent a giant house at a different beach every summer and invite the whole family to come.

It won't be a "happily ever after" story—the cycles of darkness and light continue. But have patience. Your most important struggles will be hard-fought but won well.

Endure and have faith,
Olympia

EILEEN FISHER

Clothing Designer and Entrepreneur

"You don't have to be afraid of living alone."

YOU HAVE ONLY to lay your eyes on Eileen Fisher's elegantly understated clothing to understand her talent for paring away the unessential. Now fifty-five, presiding over one of the largest privately held female-owned businesses in the country, she makes simplicity look sophisticated and the unadorned seem richly embellished.

When she greeted me at the door of her house in Irvington, New York, her company's home base, Eileen was the embodiment of this sensual purity. Her hair is uncolored, but it's such a spectacular shade of white that you instantly consider forsaking L'Oréal. She moves like the yoga devotee she is— calmly and with pleasure. She runs a large company in the fashion industry but ignores trends in favor of designs that reflect her personal values. When the teenaged Eileen and her five sisters madly primped in front of a mirror before going out, their mother used to chide them, saying, "Nobody is going to be looking at you." Now primping seems unnecessary and many people watch her.

Her employee-focused management style has won acclaim from *Fortune Small Business, Working Woman,* and the Great Place to Work Institute. Eileen shares a minimum of 10 percent of aftertax profits with her six hundred employees, gives each two thousand dollars annually to spend on education and wellness, and hosts free classes in yoga, tai chi, dance movement, and stress reduction. The company, with $195 million in sales in 2005, is also in the vanguard of social responsibility, paying close attention to the conditions of factory workers overseas who produce her clothing. It is one of the few in the United States to meet workplace standards set by Social Accountability International, a not-for-profit watchdog group in New York City.

As we talked, Eileen showed me her journal, which is filled with beautiful black lettering: long musings, stray words, quotes, and drawings. She is a seeker and has found keeping a journal, meditation, and yoga all help her reach that well of peace within herself. In her letter, written to herself in her early twenties, she had no such resources. During that period, she worked for a graphic designer, who became her boyfriend. Living with him in a dark SoHo loft in New York City, Eileen felt trapped in a narrow existence that had no way out. "I think it's the most lost I've ever been. Everything was hard. I felt depressed a lot of the time," she recalled.

One by one, her friends had fallen away because her boyfriend didn't like them. She couldn't turn to her family because her parents disapproved of their living arrangements. What's more, having boldly fulfilled a long-standing ambition by moving to New York from her home in Chicago, she didn't want to reveal herself as anything other than the strong and independent person she had always presented to the world.

Dear Eileen,

I see you in the kitchen, the only real room in that murky loft. You're there because you're trying to make space for yourself as a distinct person. You feel so negated, so erased that you're looking for a corner to call your own. But here's what you don't know: The space you're searching for isn't physical. You need psychological space. You need to know that you can be alone—that you should be alone—but you're afraid to be.

Why are you so scared? You feel you have to have a boyfriend. Without one, you feel incomplete. When you have one, you feel defined as a person. But, Eileen, that's a trap.

What I can see, almost thirty years later, is that you need time with yourself, not a friend or a beau, to figure out what your thoughts and feelings are. When you sit with yourself alone, you can't ignore them. They come screeching at you. The only way to the other side is through it. You may have to go through pain, but on the other side is the good stuff. You don't have to be afraid of living alone.

I feel so sad to think of what will happen if you don't learn this huge lesson. You'll lose pieces of yourself along the road. You know how much you love to dance? You've danced for the fun of it from the time you were tiny. You went dancing with your boyfriend in college and rocked out with friends in your dorm. All that joy is going to fall away because you're going to stop dancing for twenty years—unless you take care to listen to yourself and shepherd all the pieces of who you are through to the future. Meditation has become the best way I know to listen to myself. The gift I give you are the words I often say when I begin to meditate:

Stillness is the ground of being from which all else emerges. It is within and behind every breath, every thought, every action. It is my starting point, my resting place, the home base to which I can return again and again.

In stillness I notice how time and space disappear. All there is is the present moment and my willingness to listen . . . to allow the stillness to speak.

The stillness takes me into a realm of conscious awareness that transcends my identity as body or mind. Stillness offers an experience of being and a recognition that my being . . . my essence . . . is a part of all Being, all Essence.*

With compassion,
Eileen

*From *Meditation and Rituals for Conscious Living* by Nancy J. Napier and Carolyn Tricomi.

MACY GRAY

Singer and Songwriter

"Please yourself first . . . Everything else follows."

WHEN SINGER-SONGWRITER Macy Gray was twenty-seven, she and her husband broke up. Pregnant with their third child, she moved with her two toddlers, Aanisah, three, and Mel, two, back to her parents' five-bedroom home in Canton, Ohio, where she had grown up as Natalie McIntyre. She hadn't lived at home since she was fourteen, before going to boarding school.

The beginning of the five-month stay marked a new low in Macy's life—and a key turning point. Atlantic Records, her label, had dropped her. She was financially dependent on her parents and, searching for direction, briefly considered throwing over the music world to become a teacher or start a typing-service business for Kent State students. She and her parents argued frequently, particularly over her kids: what they would eat, where they would go, which clothes they wore.

Macy remembers feeling that an enormous weight was bearing down on her. "I felt really heavy. I like to have fun—

I wasn't used to having all this on my shoulders. I was really slow and felt like I was in a labyrinth. Everything was just so hard. I never had anything that hard," she recalls. Her letter describes the path out of the labyrinth.

Within a year, Macy signed with Epic Records and began recording *On How Life Is,* for which she received two Grammy nominations in 2000. The six-foot-tall singer with the scratchy voice and eccentric style has since released *The Id* (2001) and *The Trouble with Being Myself* (2003).

◦◦◦

Dear Nat,

You think you have made a mistake going home, but you don't know anything for sure right now. Just having Ma and Daddy around is not a negative. Even when you're fighting and you can't stand them, it's a good thing. It has to be this way to figure your life out.

You love music. That was a big part of the problem you had with your husband, who didn't support music's hold on you. Now you're trying to reclaim this essential part of yourself, but there's a hurdle you've got to get over. Stop being afraid. Stop thinking about getting back into music by giving people what they want. You've got to say "Fuck it," and please yourself first.

Nothing is gonna be harder than what you're going through now, Nat. You spent a long time trying to keep your marriage together, which kept you from a lot of things that you love. Now that you're at your parents' house, pleasing other people is not your priority. Survival is.

That'll push you, push you to reach down and pull that gutsy core of yourself up and out into the world. You'll get to the point where you're just pleasing yourself. When it's all about where your heart is, that attracts a lot of energy. Everything else follows.

You'll see I'm right when you're onstage performing. If you go out trying to make the crowd happy, your show is, like, whatever. If you perform for yourself, it's much better. Because people get that; people are attracted to that. There's nothing better than complete purity. Being completely raw always works.

Macy

~⊙~

"You don't have to be perfect."

IF YOU'RE ONE of the women whose secret Cinderella fantasies were fanned by the story of Lisa Halaby, a good-looking blond American of Arab descent who became Noor Al Hussein, queen of Jordan, when she married King Hussein in 1978, know this: She's no good at being a decorative appendage. A bit of a loner as a child and young woman, Noor's independent streak led to clashes with her strong-willed father, Najeeb Elias Halaby, president of Pan American World Airways in the late 1960s. Like many kids who came of age while Vietnam War protests roiled the country, Noor was idealistic and yearned to make a difference in the world. Unlike others, she found herself in a position to do so when she became queen at age twenty-six.

Becoming a full partner to the king took time, though. "He was so accustomed to everyone around him having an agenda. He inherited the throne in his teens and he was used to soldiering through every day without there being anyone he could turn to for help," Noor recalled when we spoke in the sitting room of her suite at Hotel Palomar in San Francisco. The bond between her and her husband was built on shared traits: inherent optimism and a drive to serve. "We both looked for reward and fulfillment outside of our own personal interests," she said.

Her most important contributions to Jordan, before her husband died of non-Hodgkin's lymphoma in 1999, were the development of several innovative programs to tackle the country's intertwined problems of poverty, unemployment, health, education, and women's rights. The programs have since helped lift tens of thousands of Jordanian women and men out of poverty. Since King Hussein's death, Noor has focused on keeping his lifelong vision alive by working on global peace efforts and building greater understanding between the East and West.

At five nine, Noor, who was wearing an embroidered turquoise tunic, black pants, and chandelier earrings on the day we met, has the carriage you'd expect of a woman who could wear a tiara without looking ridiculous, but none of the frosty attitude. She spoke in a relaxed, low-pitched voice, a half smile playing across her face as she remembered some of the details of her life with her husband. One of the most important things she said she learned from him was that if you live with your conscience and follow your instincts, you can get through anything with inner peace. In the following letter, Noor, now fifty-three, describes another lesson, one she did not learn from her self-reliant husband, but which would have helped her immensely during the winter of 1971. At the time, she was twenty and had just completed her first three semesters at Princeton University.

Dear Lisa,

I'm picking this day in your life to talk to you because it's a seminal moment. Yesterday you left Princeton and flew to Denver, landing in a snowstorm. After a slow bus ride to Aspen last night, you woke up this morning on the floor of a trailer—thanks to the generosity of two fellow travelers who knew you'd have trouble finding a boardinghouse in the middle of the night.

Today you'll pick yourself up, walk into town, and find a room. I know you feel a mixture of excitement and uncertainty as you challenge yourself to achieve independence, but rest assured this sojourn will end well. However unsettled you may feel at times, have faith in the path you are following.

Remember last fall, your first year at Princeton, when you choked during exams? You studied for days on end, not feeling you were retaining anything. Then after two exams, during which you sat there paralyzed, you went to the infirmary. The exams, which you were able to retake in the spring, were the least of the problem. Why is this happening? you wondered. You felt a stunning sense of inadequacy.

You know the ironic little twist to this? You think you're the only one flailing, but so many others at the university are, too.

You have been emotionally independent from a young age, feeling you could not depend on anyone. An eldest child, you knew your father had fairly unreachable expectations of you. You also moved every four years, so the cast of characters in your life changed regularly. Home life was often turbulent, because of your parents' difficult relationship. All of this caused you to believe that you had to be totally self-reliant.

You did just fine until you arrived at a campus in turmoil over drugs, civil rights, the Vietnam War, and the first class of women to enter Princeton in its 222-year history. There's been tremendous scrutiny of you, but no support system—no advisers or counselors—for you and your pioneering female classmates.

Lisa, I know it may be hard for you to see right now, but you're not alone. You also don't have to be perfect.

The winter season in Aspen is ideal for you. There are jobs to be had—first as a maid in a motel, then as a waitress. By the time you are ready to go back to school, in twelve months, you'll have been a part-time gofer at the Aspen Institute [a research and leadership think tank in Aspen] and worked with an environmental architect—jobs that will help shape your future career path.

This is the first time you've acted so dramatically on your instincts. In time you'll find that they always point you in the right direction. You'll also prove that you can be financially self-sufficient, which is a vital piece of knowledge for women the world over. And you will continue to challenge yourself after university, until one day a kindred spirit will inspire you to make a leap of faith in someone else—a proud descendant of the prophet Mohammad—whose indomitable faith, selfless example of service, all-embracing loving spirit, and moral courage will help you understand the path to true strength and freedom.

Noor Al Hussein

JANE KACZMAREK

Actress

~⚬~

*"True success means being a whole person,
someone with balance and compassion."*

WHEN I MET Jane Kaczmarek she was living with her husband, *The West Wing* star Bradley Whitford, and their three children in a cheerful home perched cheek by jowl with other houses in the Hollywood Hills. Tabletops were covered with family photos and walls were filled with the colorful work of painter Renee Norman. Jane's daughter, Frances, then six, happily plopped down on a piano bench to play her newest piece. The living room looked like a friendly place where kids could bounce on the sea-glass green sofas or sprawl across the scallop-edged upholstered bench. Creating such home, with crackle glazes, fabric samples, and a new bathroom, was foremost on Jane's mind when she was given a chance in 1999 to audition for the role of loudmouthed Lois in *Malcolm in the Middle*, a pilot television show about a noisy, aggressive family.

"I didn't want to audition for it. I loved being a mother. I was trying to have another baby," she explained. "But I did audition, and when I got it, I took it. We were renovating this house. I thought the money would pay for a new bathroom. But I never thought *Malcolm* would turn into this." She paused and guffawed, newly incredulous at how things had turned out. "It's like a cheesy Zen lesson. Just when you say, 'No, I don't want to do that anymore,' a big custard pie of success comes flying at your face."

The custard pie has brought Jane six Emmy nominations in a row and a smart idea about recycling the designer gowns and other finery on parade at awards shows: auction it off and give the proceeds to children's charities. She and Brad founded Clothes Off Our Back (www.clothesoffourback.org) in 2002. Among the 150 or so celebrity participants are Teri Hatcher, Ewan McGregor, Jennifer Aniston, Brad Pitt, and Charlize Theron. So far, COOB has raised nearly $1,000,000 for organizations like Cure Autism Now, Smile Train, and the Children's Defense Fund.

Using her celebrity as currency to improve the lot of others is a growing focus. "I think about what I can do with this opportunity I have to increase awareness and raise money for causes I believe in. Nothing I have found makes me feel better than raising money for children's charities," says Jane, now fifty. In her letter, she writes about a different passion—the drive to be a winner—which had her in a fierce grip throughout her twenties.

Dear Jane,

*The first thing you should know about life out here in future
land is that I'm sitting at a table on my backyard terrace, laughing
about what you're going through. As we both know, laughing is a
deadly serious matter. When you grow up with our father's
philosophy, you have to be a winner. Because, as he used to say,
other people were either afraid of you or they were laughing at you.
There was nothing in between. So when I say I'm laughing, make
no mistake: I'm not ridiculing you. I'm not enjoying your misery.
I'm laughing because your failure—or should I say your string of
failures?—is hilarious because it's so exaggerated. These—smack!—
belly flops are going to turn out to be the best things ever for you.*

*No—don't object! Let's review, Jane. You've been disgustingly
successful for an astonishingly long time. High school was a romp.
You were the lead in all the plays at college. You were accepted to
Yale's drama school, where you and another actress shared the Best
Acting prize. Then, of course, you got the best agent, moved to Los
Angeles, and got your first job from your first audition on your first
day there, at age twenty-six. You've never gone more than three
weeks without a job during your first six years as an actress. This is
not normal.*

*Let's not skip the lifestyle details. You always had a boyfriend,
the way some women always wear jewelry. Boyfriends were your
essential accessory and you broke up with one to take another if
Mr. New seemed better or more exciting. No one knew how to
recognize prime boyfriend material like you. Investment bankers
with private planes whisked you off to Nantucket. Chauffeured cars*

arrived at your apartment building equipped with champagne. This seemed normal in New York in the 1980s, but trust me, it wasn't.

You thought that all of this, the whole bubbly ride up, occurred because you worked hard for success and deserved it.

Then, at thirty-two, failure shoved its ugly head through the door.

Failure #1:

Loose Ends, *a revival at Second Stage Theatre in the spring of 1988. "There's no way I can save you," the director said the night before it opened. She put your character in a hat to make her more likable. The play was a bomb. Theater critic Mel Gusso thought you were the reason and announced it in the* New York Times.

Failure #2:

Shortly after Failure #1, you went to Toronto to film Sea of Love, *a movie with Al Pacino. You spent two weeks playing his ex-wife. Then while you were at the Williamstown Theatre Festival, you got a call telling you not to go back to finish, because you were being replaced by another actress.*

Failure #3:

You were involved with a man who was almost ten years younger than you. He seemed safe, like someone who couldn't disappoint you. Then he stopped returning your calls before you lost interest in him.

Which brings us to today. You fear that all eyes are on you—that everyone is laughing at you after all your success. Look at Miss Yale Drama School now! You feel like a piece of gum on the bottom of someone's shoe.

Okay, it's bad, I admit. I won't lie and say things are going to turn around for you quickly. But Jane, I'm going to ask you to look at the big picture. You believe you've been doing the right things, but you haven't been a good friend or even a good girlfriend.

Instead, you've been really driven and competitive because being a success has been really important to you.

Now failure is busting you wide open so that you can learn what true success means: being a whole person, someone with balance and compassion. The building blocks of success aren't plum acting jobs and beating out other actors. They are being a good friend and really loving somebody. The reason you've gone out with too many guys and dumped too many guys is that you're afraid they're going to see who you really are. And if they do, they might reject you.

Hitting bottom, which you're doing now, hurts like hell. But I promise you that some of the best things in your life will come out of it. You'll learn that it's okay to be vulnerable and really okay to say, "I don't know what I'm doing with my life." You'll develop a taste for the happiness you can have just from living a life, from mundane, everyday pleasures.

And, the best lesson of all: You'll find you can like people and let them into your world, even if they aren't big success stories. Because of that, someone different will enter your life. He won't have the trappings of success that you used to think you needed to have in a man. On your first date, he'll ride you home on the handlebars of his bike, because he has no car and can't afford to hire one. But he's really funny, smart, and has amazing integrity. Because of this horrible year, Jane, you'll be willing to pay attention to the guy you're going to marry.

From a happier future you,
Jane

⟨⟨⟨ swirl ornament ⟩⟩⟩

"Speak the truth but ride a fast horse."

DEMONIZING KITTY KELLEY, the author of contro-
versial best-selling biographies such as *His Way: The
Unauthorized Biography of Frank Sinatra* and *Jackie Oh!*, was a
surprisingly popular media sport during the election season of
2004. True, *The Family,* her two-pound tome about the Bush
dynasty, splashed down with the subtlety of a spaceship—landing only seven weeks before election day, during the most
fractious presidential race in memory. And it contains the sen-
sational charge that President Bush snorted coke with his
brother Marvin at Camp David while their father was president. But columnists and talk-show hosts could pick from so
many other blind-sourced juicy accusations flying through the
ether that the terrierlike devotion to shredding Kitty, who actually took the trouble to research her subject for years and
produce thirty-three pages of footnotes, was notable.

When I met with her in the Georgetown house that serves
as her office, I found that the dragon lady is a small, feminine

sixty-three-year-old blonde with the disconcertingly girlish habits of biting her lower lip and fluffing her blond hair over her cheeks. She lives about five blocks away, with Jonathan Zucker, her husband of thirteen years. "This is the second marriage for both of us and divinely blissful it is!" she said.

Kitty began her career in writing at the *Washington Post,* after working as a press aide for U.S. senator Eugene McCarthy, when she was twenty-eight. She was a researcher for the editorial page, which involved fetching coffee, answering phones, and gathering material for writers, as well as the chance to write an occasional op-ed piece. The highlight of those years was when executive editor Ben Bradlee got a copy of the Pentagon Papers, a Pentagon study of U.S. involvement in Vietnam, and asked her to help organize all 4,400 pages of them at his house. The *Post* began publishing them in the summer of 1971.

Kitty, whose license plate reads MEOW, says her attraction to biography stems from a fascination with people who exert an influence on our lives. Being a veteran—and a beneficiary—of the vehement attention her books generate, you'd think she'd be unruffled by criticism. But after being raked over the coals like an errant shish kebab during her two-month book tour, Kitty, who had not yet found a new book project when we talked, had a warning for her slightly younger self.

Dear Kitty,

On the eve of publication of The Family: The Real Story
of the Bush Dynasty, I'm concerned that you are thinking with
your heart and not your head. You want to present a historical
portrait of the most powerful family in the world, to be read by
both sides of the political spectrum. After four years of research and
nearly a thousand interviews, you see your book as political but not
partisan. Yet you fail to realize that it is landing in the midst of a
divisive election and will never be accepted objectively. In fact, I
think you will be pilloried for writing it.

You've been writing biographies for over twenty-five years, and
this one is by far your most daunting project because you're
delineating not just one life but many, and you're following those
lives through one hundred years of history to tell the story of
America's most influential political dynasty. Yet what makes you
think you'll be able to tell your story, which is so intimate and
revealing, without paying consequences? After all, you are writing
about a sitting president whose reach is long and formidable.

In fact, I don't know how to prepare you for the hurricane of
personal abuse to come your way—and not just from the Bush
family. You will be attacked by the White House, the Republican
National Committee, and the House majority leader. I'm not
telling you to step back from where the facts have led you, but you
must understand that few within the media will defend your
unsparing portrait, especially of the former President Bush. Matt
Lauer will criticize you on the Today show, and other television
talk-show hosts, wary of offending the Bushes, will not ask you to
appear. Even some of your Republican relatives will back away,

particularly your brother-in-law, the former CFO of Abbott Laboratories, who will refuse to attend your book party, although the proceeds will go to his wife's favorite charity.

All I can do is advise you to cling to the words of Winston Churchill, the conservative you most admire: "I do not resent criticism, even when, for the sake of emphasis, it parts for the time with reality." And don't forget that cowboy motto you have pinned to your bulletin board: "Speak the truth but ride a fast horse."

As ever,
Kitty

GERRY LAYBOURNE

CEO of Oxygen Media

⤬

*"Turn off the radio station in your head
that points out your failures."*

G ERRY LAYBOURNE RADIATES corporate composure
as she sits in her office, which is perched high above
Oxygen Media's cavernous headquarters, like the cockpit of a
jumbo jet. But it's not hard to uncover a river of feminist sub-
versiveness coursing beneath her porcelain skin. This may be
the only CEO in America who readily joins office-party
conga lines, champions women's rights daily, and discusses her
hormone therapy with subordinates at business meetings. Like
some of the programming that Oxygen, a cable TV channel
for women, has served up, Laybourne is at once intelligent and
raunchy, motherly and rebellious.

A former schoolteacher, Laybourne recast herself as a television executive in 1980 at age thirty-three, joining Viacom's
Nickelodeon network, where, she likes to say, she brought
green slime to television. Under her leadership, Nickelodeon
became a top-rated, award-winning cable service and a huge

moneymaker. After sixteen years, Laybourne left Nickelodeon in 1996 to become president of Disney/ABC Cable Networks, responsible for Disney's cable programming and its ABC subsidiary, as well as for developing future television programming for cable.

She departed from Disney in order to start Oxygen in 1998. Difficult as it is to believe about a woman who ultimately persuaded investors to pony up $600 million to launch the new channel, raising money cowed Gerry, she told me when I met with her. "I did one thing for sixteen years, which was to be a really good corporate executive who built a brand and who lived inside the rules. I broke as many as I could, but I was basically a good corporate citizen," she said, fixing me with a level gaze as she probed beneath her success story. "If I'd had the courage to go out and get backing earlier in my career, I could have created a brand that could never be taken away from me or my audience."

Now a fifty-seven-year-old grandmother, Gerry has nursed Oxygen through some nearly disastrous missteps. The company, which produces original programming such as *Girls Behaving Badly* and shows reruns like *Xena: Warrior Princess,* turned its first quarterly profit in 2004 and expected to reach 60 million homes by the end of 2005.

Here, Gerry writes to herself at age forty-nine, regarding the pivotal decision to leave Nickelodeon.

◦◦◦

Dear Gerry:

Here you are in a nice "safe" corporate job, protected from financial woes by big, powerful corporate parents. How naïve are you? You've spent sixteen years successfully pitching investment opportunities within one company. The road has hardly been easy. To get funding, you had to compete with all the other internal divisions, which believed that their ideas were as valid as yours for building the company's future. Internal competition is alive and well, and sibling rivalry is oh so much fun.

But you actually know nothing about the world of venture capital, private equity, or banking. You think you're an entrepreneur. You think you "own" Nickelodeon. But you know nothing about being a real entrepreneur. And you haven't done the first thing to find out how you could actually be one.

You are about to have the courage to leave an enterprise that you love and people whom you cherish. For what? To walk into a new corporation that doesn't have a history of supporting entrepreneurs, with only a "promise" that you'll be allowed to develop new things.

Open your eyes. You're walking into a Wall Street–driven, quarterly measured corporate culture that hasn't really bought into your ideas. Your soon-to-be bosses don't understand how much your own sense of success is defined by independence and a sense of creative freedom.

Wake up. If you ventured outside a big "safe" corporation, you'd discover infinite sources of money. We live in a capitalist society, where investors hunger for good ideas and people with proven track records. You think that only inside a big corporation you'll find ready capital and solid support. Raising money isn't that big a mystery, but it is the final business frontier for women. We know how to do all the steps that go into it—have an idea, figure out how it would work, discover who would want it, understand what the business climate is, and develop a long-term plan.

All that's missing is the seed money. Why does it seem to you, of all people, to be a bigger hurdle than any other business obstacle? I can tell you right now that all the other things are much harder. Setting the vision, building the brand—that's brain surgery. Raising money is nothing compared with those tasks.

Start by thinking about who can help you actualize your vision. Talk to people you know and trust about bankers and investors whom they know and trust, and set up meetings. If you don't know someone who can introduce you to bankers, organizations like Springboard (www.Springboardenterprises.org) and the American Woman's Economic Development Corporation (www.AWED.org) can help you learn about the process.

And when you do land a meeting with a banker, here are some rules to keep in mind:

Rule #1:

Don't feel too grateful that they took the meeting. They need good ideas, good people, and good prospects as much as you need their money.

Rule #2:

Be choosy. If they make you feel stupid—jargon abounds— move on.

Rule #3:

Gather the facts, analyze the pros and cons, and evaluate the people who are offering you money. Don't ignore your intuition. It's your best gift and your most reliable tool!

Rule #4:

Raise as much money as you can and then spend cautiously—or raise cautiously and spend cautiously. The key here is that cautious spending is the way to go. Everyone makes early mistakes about people and projects. A slow start is your friend.

Rule #5, the Golden Rule:

Above all, remember to be your own best friend. Turn off the radio station in your head that points out your failures.

> *Love,*
> *Gerry (eight years later)*

REBECCA LOBO

Olympic Basketball Athlete

⌒⊘⌒

"You can pick and choose."

I T ' S N O S U R P R I S E that Rebecca Lobo is tall (six four). Her
height and a remarkable way with a basketball have shaped
her life. She is the all-time leading scorer in Massachusetts high
school basketball history, among both girls and boys. At the
University of Connecticut, her team won the national championship and she was named the tournament's Most Outstand-
ing Player. She played for the 1996 U.S. Olympic basketball
team and in 1997 helped New York Liberty reach the
WNBA's first championship game.

But what gets lost amid the string of stunning athletic
achievements is Rebecca's smile. As I discovered when I met
with her in her Simsbury, Connecticut, town house, a court-
side view doesn't let you see how it starts slowly, a bit shyly,
grows, and keeps expanding after most people would have
reached maximum wattage. Then it hits you: She's beautiful.

Now thirty and married to *Sports Illustrated* writer Steve
Rushin, Rebecca became a mother to Siobhan Rose Rushin

on Christmas morning in 2004. "I adore being a mom. It is more rewarding than I ever imagined. She's been a sweet baby since she was born and it already seems like she has her own sense of humor," she said. Last year, Rebecca worked for ESPN, broadcasting the WNBA games, but Steve and Siobhan were able to accompany her on all trips last summer, except for one. "I really enjoy doing the broadcasting but will always, always put motherhood first. So, if we have more children, I might have to give up the broadcasting," she said, looking forward to a bigger family.

Nine years ago, this happy life seemed like it might be impossible to achieve. Here is what Rebecca would say to herself at twenty-one.

⌒⌒

Dear Rebecca,

Your head is spinning. Basketball has taken you further than you could have ever dreamed. UConn won the national title and now, unbelievably, you've earned a spot on the team that will go to the Olympics. You're only twenty-one, yet you've been on the Late Show *with David Letterman and* Live *with Regis and Kathy Lee. Young girls hand you roses and send you school reports they've written about you. Your high school in Southwick, Massachusetts, is located on Rebecca Lobo Way. It's never happened in women's basketball before, but somehow you're a celebrity—recognized wherever you go.*

The attention feels like a wave that has carried you up to the top of its curl and just doesn't stop cresting. It's no wonder that you sometimes wish you could slink back into some sort of anonymity.

Your family gives you the kind of refuge and anchor you need. But, Rebecca, can't you see that your boyfriend doesn't?

I see what's happening and I'm puzzled. You're traveling the country and the world for the first time with your team, but you feel like you're on a leash—worried about going out to dinner with your teammates in case you miss his call. Or, more to the point, worried that missing his call will trigger another fight that ends with tears running down your cheeks. You don't enjoy conflict and arguments, but they've become a regular part of your phone calls and conversations with your boyfriend. He's a good guy, yes, and he makes you laugh. But for some reason, he can't trust you. You're both young and you just aren't right for each other.

This is the first real boyfriend you've had. I think you're expecting it to be like the only relationship you've known—your parents'. They have their irritated moments, but they love each other to death and they trust each other completely.

Why isn't your relationship like that? Here is where your best traits, your determination and persistence, are working against you. You can't make this work. You have to find the right person.

Don't spend nearly two years anticipating his next blowup. Say good-bye to your boyfriend now. You'll form much closer relationships with your teammates. Your friends won't be given short shrift. You'll get to fully experience traveling to China, Australia, and Siberia. You'll get to see as much as you want of your family when you go back home, rather than feeling pressured to devote every instant to him.

There will be a lot of terrific men who will have an interest in you. You're just as special as your family has taught you all along, Rebecca. You can pick and choose. Your future husband is a writer who will devote a funny, adulatory column to describe the way he fell in love with you. At age twenty-one, your boyfriend is making you cry. At thirty, you'll say about your marriage, "It couldn't be more perfect."

You warm my heart,
Rebecca

◦○◦

*"The universe is like a pension plan.
It will match your investment."*

BETWEEN THE AGES of twenty-three and twenty-six,
Camryn Manheim was engaged in daily warfare—or so
it felt. In the fall of 1984, she arrived at New York University's Tisch School of the Arts straight from the University of
California at Santa Cruz, bursting with confidence about her
plans to become an actress. Within months, her professors began to upbraid her about her size and pressure her to lose
weight.

For three years, her life—as she remembers it—consisted of
putting on invisible boxing gloves every morning before she
walked out the door of her loft apartment on the Lower East
Side. Teachers regularly questioned her about her weight in
front of her classmates, often suggesting that being overweight
proved she wasn't dedicated. "The message was 'Your body is
your instrument. You show a lack of commitment to your art,
because you have no respect for your body,' " recalls Camryn.
The verbal attacks were not only humiliating but threatening,

she says, because the Tisch School uses a "cut" system to elim-
inate students whom they believe are not a good match for the
program. Seven out of twenty-nine students in Camryn's class
were eventually axed. With the guillotine ready to slice down
at any moment, Camryn felt powerless to defend herself much
of the time.

She found solace writing in her journals and playing her
guitar in her "room," an area sectioned off by huge curtains and
decorated with tapestries, candles, and photographs. A beat-up
Honda CB650 motorcycle, which she rode around Manhattan
for four years, also supplied periodic release from criticism. "I
would put myself in positions of power when I could. I didn't
know anyone who wouldn't want a ride on the back of a motorcycle through the streets of Greenwich Village," she remembers. Since those early days as a struggling actress and
student, Camryn has won an Emmy (1998) and a Golden
Globe (1999) for her role as defense attorney Ellenor Frutt on
ABC's drama *The Practice*. Some of her other film and television credits include *An Unfinished Life*, *Dark Water*, *Happiness*,
Romy and Michelle's High School Reunion, *Elvis*, *Will & Grace*,
Two and a Half Men, *Chicago Hope*, and *The Tenth Kingdom*.

The daughter of activist parents, who congratulated her
when she called from jail after being arrested for participating
in a pro-choice rally, Camryn says her own donations of time
and money are genetic requirements. She champions people
with disabilities, particularly the deaf, as well as the American
Civil Liberties Union, local family clinics, and Planned Par-
enthood, among others. "I honestly feel I'm happier than most
people, but I sometimes feel I live on a foundation of sorrow
because of what's going on here on this planet," she explains.

One potent antidote is a small boy named Milo Jacob Manheim, born to Camryn on March 6, 2001, when she was

thirty-nine. Normally a font of self-expression, she falls momentarily silent when asked what its like to have a son. Then she says, "It's heaven on a stick. Nothing better." The letter that follows is a message back to the free-spirited, motorcycle-riding Camryn, who was suffocating under a blanket of disapproval at New York University.

◦◦◦

Dear Camryn,

I know you know pretty much everything. I know no one really understands you. I know my input will be scrutinized by your skeptical eye. But on the off chance that something I say rings true and real for you, I'm going to give it the good old college try.

Trust me when I say it gets better. It gets a whole hell of a lot better. Not that people change—those idiot "authority figures" who judge and criticize you, the assholes who limit you and tell you that your dreams are too big.

Unfortunately, that doesn't change that much. What does change, what will change for you, is that the fighter in you, the warrior, the boxer, the avenger will accumulate the weapons that will lead you to victory. I know you're a pacifist; I know you're not going to take anyone out or down. The weapons I'm talking about aren't weapons of mass destruction (because as we all know they don't exist) . . . but they are weapons of the heart and soul. Like confidence, and wit and audacity. Like speaking your mind, standing up for your beliefs, believing in yourself. These weapons are unbeatable. No one can spar with your confidence. You are the only one who can defeat it.

I know it's hard to imagine being happy when there is so much suffering in the world. And it's important to recognize the global suffering. But you know it's possible to feel joy. I've seen you feel it. Like when you see a play that you loved so much, you're jealous you weren't in it. Or when you hear a new Neil Young album, or ride your motorcycle with a cute boy on the back over the Brooklyn Bridge on a hot summer night. Those things are joyous. If you could string as many moments of joy together as closely as possible, then I'd say, it gets a whole lot better.

The universe is like a pension plan. It will match your investment. If you put 10 percent of your potential in, it will match that 10 percent and you will be operating at 20 percent of your possibilities. But if you put in 100 percent, the global collective will kick in and give you an additional 100 percent back on your return. It's the best investment plan I know—being proactive about your life.

The thing is, Camryn, life isn't a dress rehearsal. We don't get any do-overs. You've got to make the days count—all of them.

So go kick some ass. Don't take no for an answer. Work hard, play hard, fight hard, and love hard. Break some rules and raise a little hell. And at the end of every day, ask yourself if you have any regrets. I guarantee you, you will rarely regret the things you did do, and mostly regret the things you didn't do. So do it. Do it all. Learn French. Get a piano. Write your one-person show. Fall in love more often. Love the journey, not just the result.

When you read this letter, and realize you already know it all, do me a favor and tuck it in your back pocket for a rainy day. It might have more meaning after it's been in your pocket for a few years, all worn and tattered, and you have to strain to read it through the faded ink.

> Your comrade in arms,
> Camryn

MARY MATALIN

Political Commentator

"There really is not one true way to career success."

M<small>ARY</small> <small>MATALIN</small> <small>MAY</small> have served two presidents and a vice president, hosted shows on CNN and CNBC, and been chief of staff for the Republican National Committee, but if you talk to her, it's not a shock to learn that she once studied to get a beautician's license. She's got an easy, down-to-earth manner that would make anyone feel at home. A fast talker with wide-ranging mind, she'll squeeze in a parenthetical comment on spirituality and a quick segue about parenting while answering a question about her youth. As we talked, it quickly became clear that Mary is a world-champion chatter, particularly, she confesses, with her sister Renie.

The most absorbing recent development in Mary's life has been motherhood. A dedicated career gal, Mary mounted a poster that read OOPS, I FORGOT TO HAVE KIDS behind her desk while working in President George H. W. Bush's reelection campaign. Her plans didn't change after marrying her political archrival, James Carville, who had been chief campaign strategist for Bill Clinton, in 1993. But five months later, she became accidentally pregnant at forty-one. She was broken-hearted after having a miscarriage, but later she had two daughters.

Though Matty, eleven, and Emma, nine, are no longer babies, Mary finds she grows more fascinated, rather than less, by the process of raising children. So she quit her job at the White House in President Bush's midterm to enjoy full-time mommyhood spiced with, oh, a few hundred other political and activist projects. Mary says being a parent has taught her a few tricks for managing some of the unruly parts of her life. "When I wake up with nighttime fears and my heart starts racing, I now treat that person in me as having an annoying temper tantrum. The worst thing you can do with kids is respond to their tantrum. So I don't respond to those irrational fears," she explains.

To Mary, one of motherhood's most important perks is the chance it gives her to reconnect with memories of her mother, who died of cancer at fifty, when Mary was just twenty-six. Shocked and devastated, she "began a career at warp speed, with no plans or any idea what to do with my brand-new political science degree. My only goal was to leave *no space* for the choking pain and grief," she writes in *Letters to My Daughters.* Now fifty-three, she addresses herself in her late twenties and early thirties, when she was career-obsessed.

◦◦◦

Dear Mary:
    You are launching a career and a life overwhelmed by advice books, counselors, and friends. Stop and think where you have always gotten your best advice, no matter what the topic . . . your

*mama. Missing Ma should not cause you to dismiss what she taught
you about work and the world. Your fast track may not look like
her beaten path, but her life lessons apply to any and all of your life
labors. You may have traveled different roads, but you started from
the same place: ethnic, Midwest, girls of a "certain era."*

*So lets review Ma's basic lessons for work and play—which is the
first lesson: Work should not be work. You should love your job.*

*When you are looking for work, don't overdo the career
counseling. A career path plan can become a career-crippling
pathology. Contrary to all the advice books and columns, there
really is not one true way to career success—at least not for people
like you. Your compass is not set to conventional methods and
measurements, such as setting long-term goals, advancing
methodically through promotions, raises, and titles. You are high-
strung, easily bored, hyperenergized. You have a short but deep
attention span. Sure, you wouldn't list those on a job application as
"skills," but they are characteristics that suit fast-paced and intense
projects. You may flit from project to project, but a lifetime of fun
and interesting projects adds up to a career just as sound as the
plodding ones you read about. Devise your own career template.
Corollary: There is also no career "clock." Move along at your own
pace.*

*More important for any life situation: Appreciate your abilities
and trust your instincts. Just because you haven't done something
doesn't mean you can't. You can learn anything and hire experts. A
fancy pedigree, or even innate genius, is no substitute for the work
ethic and common sense you have.*

*Conversely, no amount of hard work or acquired expertise can
overcome a "bad fit." If your instincts are saying,* **Something's
wrong in paradise,** *then there probably is a problem. Do not
ignore tugs of trepidation or constant discomfort, even if you
cannot put your finger on exactly what's bugging you. There are*

many reasons the "perfect" job may not be so perfect in a day-to-day situation, which is, after all, how we live our lives. Maybe you misjudged your interest, or your colleagues. This doesn't mean if you have a few bad days you should pack it in. It means pay attention to low-grade dissatisfaction before it turns into a potential self-destruction. On the other hand, if your instincts compel you to what appears on the surface the dumbest, zaniest, absolutely most undoable project, take a hard look at it. Your instincts are early indicators of both good and bad.

Many people need more concrete rules than you do. Don't worry if you are pushing forty, or even fifty, and you are still wondering what you want to be when you grow up! Trust yourself, believe in yourself, and hang in there for the ride.

Love,
Mary

HEATHER MILLS McCARTNEY

Activist

"Learn to say no."

IF ALL YOU know about Heather Mills McCartney is that she married the cute Beatle, it would be easy to dismiss her activism as the short-lived, millimeter-deep variety embraced by some celebrities. But, as her letter suggests, compassion was knit into Heather's character during childhood. Her mother split from her father when Heather was nine, leaving her and her siblings, older brother Shane and younger sister Fiona, to take the brunt of her authoritarian father's verbal and physical abuse. After her father landed in prison, when she was a teenager, Heather moved to London to live with her mother, but she left home soon after. Over the years, she worked in a carnival as a cleaner and ride operator, in a jewelry store, behind a wine bar, at a tanning salon, and, for a time, lived roughly under the arches of the Waterloo Bridge.

This bumpy beginning fueled Heather's resolve to succeed on her own. She became a distributor of two products, built them into small businesses, and sold them—all while launching a modeling career. After marrying in 1989, at twenty-one, she started a successful modeling and photographer's agency, which she later sold. Even as she established herself, she frequently reached out to poor, abused, or needy people she came across. "If I'm on the street and see a person in need, I'm the person who goes over to help. It's something I must do," says Heather.

After a divorce in her early twenties, Heather settled in northern Yugoslavia (now Slovenia), which was rent by civil war in 1991. Seeing the effects of this firsthand, Heather modeled to raise funds for refugee centers, hospitals, and homes for war victims, eventually moving back to London. Then, one summer day in 1993, a police motorcycle crashed into her, crushing ribs, puncturing a lung, fracturing her pelvis, and causing her to lose her left leg below the knee. The stump was slow to heal and required a second amputation of several inches. When it finally did mend, Heather characteristically decided this particular piece of adversity was sent her way so that she could become a charitable supplier of artificial limbs to amputees, particularly land-mine and war victims.

Her work has helped thousands of adults and children around the world, and it led Heather to campaign for land-mine removal. Her achievements in Croatia and Phnom Penh, Cambodia, earned her a 1996 Nobel Prize nomination, as well as other awards and recognition. Heather and her husband, Paul McCartney, became patrons of Adopt-A-Minefield, which aims to raise enough funds to clear all minefields in the world.

Her letter is written to herself between the ages of seventeen and twenty.

Dear H,

Learn to say no. From the day your mum left you as a child and your father controlled and abused your life, you've been on a mission to "save" each and every disadvantaged person you come across. You got into a brawl to protect a bullied, acne-covered teenager at school and it led to your own suspension. You repeatedly went to the rescue of a violently abused mother down the street, but she never left her abusive husband.

You feel physically compelled to help others, down to the sensation in your stomach. Helping is good—it's important—but at what cost? Hours, days, and weeks away from your family and friends.

Find a balance. Chose whom you say yes to and whom you say no to. Giving yourself completely can be damaging to you and your family. Never give up that drive and passion to help, but don't always prioritize a stranger in need over your own family. Try helping that person once, maybe twice, but don't give up your house to move them in, disrupting everyone else's life in the household.

Do what you're doing because it does make a difference. At the same time, remember that some people need help but that they must also learn to help themselves. Some can even resent you for your know-it-all attitude. What's helpful to them one day can be "Miss Bossy Boots" the next.

So go ahead and learn to say no sometimes. You should stand by someone for a certain amount of time, but if all they do is take,

take, take, you have to let go and get rid of the vampires.
Stop being their savior and be your own. Equilibrium in life is
everything.

Love,
Yourself

TRISH McEVOY

Makeup Artist and Founder of Trish McEvoy, Ltd.

∽◦◯◦∼

"The key elements in life are time and people."

CHRISTMAS AT TRISH McEvoy's Fifth Avenue apartment in New York City looks nothing like the breakneck-paced green-and-red extravaganza I'm familiar with. When I visited her in late December, the elevator opened up to a large foyer trimmed, like the rest of the apartment, with generous cream-painted moldings, cornices, and woodwork. Rose and ivory colors saturated the living room and adjacent sitting room, in which Trish McEvoy, Ltd., scented candles burned at 9:00 A.M. White lilies and greenery burst out of wall niches in the living room. A ten-foot evergreen swathed in white and cream decorations stood by a window, which looked out over the bare tree tops of Central Park.

I took it all in and decelerated, albeit a little rustily. A Maltese named Cutie barked importantly at me until I sat down. Then Trish bounced in to meet me. The fifty-five-year-old owner of a cosmetics and personal-care products company with more than 220 stores in the United States and Europe looks like she could shop in the preteen department. Tiny, she occasionally had to hitch up her jeans as we talked. Her face looked completely bare—which she later assured me it was not—and fresh. Surely, I thought, there must be a wart in this exceptional display of beauty and graciousness.

Within minutes, Trish banished the notion. Not for nothing do clients of more than thirty years regularly call her to apply their makeup. Unpretentious and accepting, Trish has a talent for friendship in her business and outside of it. She maintains relationships with many of the hundreds of women who held house parties for her when she began selling her cosmetics in the 1970s. She's been married for twenty-five years to Ron Sherman, a dermatologist, with whom she opened up the Dr. Ronald Sherman/Trish McEvoy Skincare Center in New York City in 1978. "I believe in looong relationships," she said.

Her letter contains a message about one of her longest, deepest relationships—with her remarkable mother-in-law, Sydell Sherman, who died in May 2004 at the age of ninety-six. Syd, as everyone called her, lived on her own, without help, until her death. She never used a walker and was always immaculately put together. "To me, she was a perfect person. She was totally self-reliant. She lived for her children and treated me like one of them," said Trish.

Syd's Fifth Avenue apartment was in the same building as the Dr. Ron Sherman/Trish McEvoy Skincare Center. So Trish and Ron routinely visited Syd after work, and often popped in during the day. During summer weekends, the trio would head out to the couple's Southampton home, settling in with a treat that Syd especially delighted in: dinner at Robert's, a local restaurant. "She loved it because when she was a young girl she loved reading the society pages and she stayed interested in current events. And in this restaurant she would see the people who were people she may have read about in the newspaper. When she'd spot one, oh, she got such a kick out of it," recalled Trish.

Hoping that Syd would agree to move in with them, Trish and Ron renovated a bedroom and bathroom in their apartment in 2003. Syd looked over the rooms, pronounced them "very nice," but declined repeated invitations to stay for a night or two. Then one spring day, Trish impulsively decided to skip her exercise-training session and go over to her mother-in-law's apartment. Syd was not doing well. "I said, 'Why don't you come over to the apartment?' She said, 'I think tonight I'm going to stay over,' " recalled Trish. "I knew the end was near—and she knew it."

Syd died the next day. Trish's letter is to herself one year before Syd's death.

∾⊚∾

Dear Trish,

You adore Syd. After three decades of feeling the blaze of her love, she's become so essential to you. Before she married, she took care of her four sisters. Then she took care of her family, and for years that has included you. She has the knack of focusing on her loved ones without interfering. She's not a big advice giver and she never judges. She knows what to say—and what not to say. If you utter a criticism of someone, she'll say gently, "Look at it through their eyes."

You spend lots of time with her, at her apartment, on Long Island, or just sitting in the park, watching the artists and illustrators at work. She asks, "Why do you want to spend time with an old lady?" You've asked her a lot of questions about her life and her thoughts: "How did the war affect you?" "When were you allowed to date?" "How did you get the kids to take piano?" *Syd responds:* "Stop asking me those questions. What difference does it make?"

But it does—it makes a difference. The key elements in life are time and people: What are you spending your time on and whom are you spending it with? Every minute that goes by can't be reclaimed, relived, reworked. You know this already, Trish—but not the way you'll know it, as if it's etched into your bones, a year from now.

Keep asking Syd those questions. Ask even more. Ask about the time before you knew her, when she was growing up, starting her family, raising her kids. Spend even more time with her. Before long, your chance to know more about her will be gone. If you ask now, while you have the chance, your rich relationship can grow even deeper.

And spend more time just being with her. Later, it's going to kill you to think of her sitting in that chair in her apartment for hours, with no one. Soon the amazing, tenacious, lively woman you've known won't be able to get out to walk on the street or go to the park. She's going to weaken, because of her lung condition. As you know, she refuses to watch television during the day. And she won't take a nap, for fear she'll never get up again. So she sits alone, reading biographies.

The way you look at it, being with Syd isn't a duty. It's a joy. So be there, even more than you already are. Give yourself the gift of enjoying her a little more than you do already.

You have a term of endearment for Syd that goes back to when your sister-in-law's son became a father for the first time. Baby Amanda became your sister-in-law's sole focus. So you were inspired to give Syd a new answer when she wondered why you

*wanted to spend so much time with an old lady. You told her,
"Mom, you're my Amanda."*

*You're going to be so glad you spoke your heart. You've been a
true daughter to her. You'll never have to worry that Syd didn't
know how much you loved her.*

> *Love,*
> *Trish*

Barcelona 92

SHANNON MILLER

Olympic Gymnast

❦

"Mistakes can help you learn."

IN 1992, FIFTEEN-year-old Shannon Miller was bedecked in more medals than any other American athlete at the Olympic Games: five. Four years later, she surprised observers who thought she was too old to compete by winning the first American gold on the balance beam and helping the U.S. women's team earn its first gold medal. Today, she is still the most decorated American gymnast, male or female, with seven Olympic medals and nine World Championship medals.

Years of heady attention climaxed after the 1996 games, causing Shannon to face a void. "I felt like I had to get to the next goal. I had to do something big," she remembers, speaking to me from Boston, where she is pursuing a law degree from Boston College.

The pressure to produce an extraordinary next step dogged her during a post-Olympic tour. She recalls sitting at a table in an office-supply store and signing autographs. It seemed as though every autograph seeker asked her what she was going to do next. "As people kept asking me that question, I felt worse and worse and worse because I didn't know the answer," she says. "I wondered what answer I could give them that would make them happy."

She finally came up with the next big thing—marriage—which she now believes was a mistake for her. Twenty-nine-year-old Shannon writes to herself between the ages of nineteen, after the 1996 Olympics, and twenty-two, when she got married.

❧

Dear Shannon,

Having forty extra hours a week is scaring you. You're used to a schedule that governs every single second of your time. You have no idea how to do nothing, but you don't know how to fill the time, either.

The reason is simple. You don't know who Shannon Miller is— your preferences, what's important to you, what you dislike. Of course, you do know about the passion that has completely shaped your life: gymnastics. But ever since you won your first medals at fifteen, gymnastics has called for a whole new level of perfection. You realized that people were listening to what you were saying and watching what you were doing. You wanted to be a good role model and you thought they expected you to be without faults.

But actually, you've taken it too far. Afraid to say the wrong thing, afraid to hurt anyone's feelings, afraid to voice your opinion. You exaggerated people's expectations, so you haven't allowed yourself to make mistakes. Yet mistakes can help you learn. Try to figure out who you are as a person, Shannon, and don't just be what everybody else wants you to be.

Looking for the next big thing without understanding what you want out of life will lead you to get married too young. You'll believe that marriage means leaving behind your passion for gymnastics, as if it was a childish plaything. But eventually you'll realize that you're not happy when you get up every day. You'll begin to think about what elements need to be in your life for you to be happy.

Some of those things you'll have to learn from scratch: sitting at the window, watching the snow come down; playing with your dog. You spent so much time getting to the next goal, you forgot to look at things along the way. Other parts of a happy life you'll rediscover: being close to your family and keeping gymnastics in your life. Just because your life changes doesn't mean that your deepest passions have to.

With love,
Shannon

SHELLEY MORRISON

Actress

∽◦◦∽

"You only know what you know of life at any given point."

S HELLEY MORRISON HAS perhaps the most satisfying
role on *Will & Grace*. As Rosario Salazar, a flinty El Sal-
vadoran maid, she's the character who gets to skewer the
swollen sense of superiority that inflates her boss, Karen
Walker. Though her role was originally planned for only one
episode, Shelley played Rosario with such poker-faced skill
that she earned a permanent spot on the NBC hit.

Now sixty-nine, Shelley has performed in dozens of plays
and made guest appearances on more than 150 televisions
shows and in fifteen feature films during a career of more than
forty years. Older TV fans are most likely to remember her as
Sister Sixto opposite Sally Field in the 1960s series *The Flying
Nun*. Despite the show's eventual success, that period of her
life was one of her toughest because it coincided with her father's illness and death. In 1967, Shelley had just completed
the pilot for *The Flying Nun*. While she was waiting to hear if
it would be picked up, her father, Morris Mitrani, had a series
of minor strokes, one of which landed him in the hospital. Af-

ter undergoing a series of tests, he had a devastating stroke, which incapacitated him.

To help her mother with her father's care, Shelley moved back home and became a key practical and financial support during the medical crisis. During the ten months her father was at Midway Hospital in Los Angeles, she would take her mother, Dena, to the hospital at 6:00 A.M., get to work by 7:00 A.M., and return at noon. She then went back to work, returning to the hospital again at about 8:00 P.M. In his room, she and her mother would wash and shave Morris. They got nurses at the understaffed facility to move him every half hour, bribing them with Green Stamps, and stayed with him until midnight, before returning home to household chores.

"With very little sleep, I'd get up every morning and do it all again," she says of those months, when *The Flying Nun* began production. "Thank goodness I was a quick study! When did I have time to learn my lines? In makeup."

Despite this devotion, when Shelley's father died of pneumonia in 1968, when she was thirty, she felt terrible guilt. "It took me a long time after my father passed to accept it. I was beating myself up, asking, 'Did I do everything that I could have done?' " she says. Her letter is to that grief-stricken young woman.

❧

Dear Rachelica,

Your father was your rock and an incredible, wonderful, kind human being. This crushing sense of guilt you have about his death makes no sense. Think—you took on a new show, cared for your father, your aunts, and your mother, and made sure all the medical bills were paid.

But guilt doesn't listen to a rational argument. So here's what I would say. You only know what you know of life at any given point. You can't beat yourself up for what you should have done if you weren't equipped with the knowledge at that time.

You're also involved in a hurtful relationship. You know that wonderful line from the film Sunday Bloody Sunday? *"Sometimes nothing is better than just anything." That's true about this guy. Now that your father is gone, you're the head of the family. It's time to get your act together and start honoring yourself.*

Don't worry, you're going to find help with this. You'll discover a therapist who will help you immensely. It will be traumatic but you'll talk it out. Writing will also help you purge—you'll call it "bloodletting."

Shelley, you know that we have guardian angels. We really do, and it's okay to ask for help. In fact, they like it. They want you to be happy, to function, and to be able to leave this planet a better place than you found it.

Blessings and love,
Shelley

MARILYN CARLSON NELSON

CEO of Carlson Companies

"If you find yourself too far out of balance, make a change."

W E'VE BEEN TRAINED to think of heiresses as spoiled airheads with small dogs. Marilyn Carlson Nelson, whose father, Curtis L. Carlson, founded Carlson Companies, a travel and hotel empire, handily breaks rank.

By the age of twenty-two, she had earned a degree from Smith College, studied at the Sorbonne in Paris and the Institute des Hautes Etudes Economiques Politiques in Geneva, and begun work as a securities analyst at Paine Webber. In her late thirties and early forties, she honed her leadership skills through her involvement with community causes, leading her to the presidency of the Minneapolis chapter of United Way as well as the chairmanship of a task force that successfully wooed the Super Bowl to Minnesota in 1992. Since 1997, the year before she succeeded her father as chief executive officer at Carlson, the private company's sales under all Carlson brands have grown 30 percent, to $26.1 billion, through 2004, making it bigger than FedEx, which was number 78 on *Fortune*'s 2005 list of the five hundred largest public companies.

This list of accomplishments looks seamless. But, like many mothers, Marilyn agonized over her role after she had three children and was pregnant with her fourth. Her husband, a surgeon, urged her to quit her job to be at home with the kids. "I went through one of those emotional periods where you have to face up to your choices. I realized that if I wanted to be the best possible parent, the right thing was to be at home," Marilyn remembers. Now sixty-seven, she gives her twenty-eight-year-old self career advice shortly after that decision, when she was still unsettled about what it portended.

Today her children, Diana, Wendy, and Curtis, are grown. Her daughter Juliet died in a car accident in 1985, while in college. "When healing from the shock of my nineteen-year old daughter's untimely death, I took solace in the fact that we had spent so much time together. My choice to first raise my family felt affirmed in a sad but poignant way," she says.

✒

Dear Marilyn,

You have ambitious dreams that seem to include every possibility under the sun. You want to be a mother. You want exactly four children. You also want to be a political leader or a diplomat. You want to serve as a community leader and you want one day to have a meaningful role in your family's business at Carlson Companies.

Those who know you wonder why you think you can do it all. How can you possibly reconcile all those dreams into one lifetime? You think that you can. So there are moments when you feel frustrated because it isn't all coming together neatly. Reality, you discover, can be a mighty foe of dreams. Maybe you should let some go.

Maybe that's what you've done by deciding to stay home. Deep in your heart, you know that your decision to stop working now that you're pregnant with your fourth child is the right decision. So stop wasting energy wishing for the excitement of a career when you've committed yourself to being at home. Here's a little test: Ask yourself, What will I regret most if I never get it done? Being at home at this moment matters to you most. The main thing, as they say, is keeping the main thing the main thing. So do it.

Here's a tip. While you're spending more time at home, get involved in volunteer work that allows you to make a real difference in your community on issues you feel passionately about, like racial equality and children's development. You just may find that you'll get more exposure and visibility and satisfaction from your volunteer efforts than you could receive from an orderly corporate climb.

Later there will be time to move to the next dream. What I know now is that women can actually come pretty close to having it all, but you just can't have it all every day. It may need to be sequenced.

You'll find it's still possible to hold an executive position in the family business later on, if that's your choice. But remember, if you choose to do that, you are in essence choosing to compete in the corporate version of the Olympics. And, just like an Olympic athlete in training, don't expect much work/life balance.

And always keep in mind that these are choices you make. Don't blame anyone else. You have to be personally accountable. If you find yourself too far out of balance, make a change.

And, remember those political aspirations? Well, you will be asked to run for governor or senator someday. And then you will have to face up to the fact that while it would be a fine thing to be a governor or senator, you don't actually want to do what governors and senators have to do. I hate to be the one to tell you this, but you're just not patient enough. So rather than sport an impressive title, you'll decline to run.

But I promise you that you won't be disappointed in that decision if your real dream is to make an impact, to make a measurable difference. If you look at every stage of your life as an opportunity to do that, your effectiveness will increase, your reputation will grow, and extraordinary possibilities will present themselves, including some that you could never have dreamed for yourself.

So you see, Marilyn, in the end, you weren't really dreaming about titles or positions or even about being a wife or a mother. Rather, you were dreaming about living the life that would complete you—one of purpose and passion and always with the intention to make a difference.

Let it unfold,
Marilyn

INGRID   NEWKIRK

Founder of People for the Ethical Treatment of Animals

◦◦◦

"You've listened to what's in your heart."

YOU UNDOUBTEDLY KNOW People for the Ethical Treatment of Animals (PETA) because of its graphic in-your-face tactics. A recent global campaign against KFC stores involved a display of fake chickens, phony blood dripping from their slit throats, with signs that read THE COLONEL'S SE-CRET RECIPE: LIVE SCALDING, PAINFUL DEBEAKING, CRIPPLED CHICKENS. I was prepared to encounter a shrill, angry woman when I met Ingrid Newkirk, fifty-six, a native of Britain, who cofounded the not-for-profit organization in 1980 and has been its president ever since. Instead, I found a tall, slender woman with a pixie face and a self-effacing manner.

Wearing a pastel pink sweater and scarf, Ingrid spoke passionately about her cause. Her whispery voice became tremulous with grief when she described the expressions on dogs' faces as the giant cage they were in was lowered into a drowning pool, a scene she witnessed in Taiwan. "Nobody wants to die and nobody can realize this is happening to them. And they are all horrified. Their eyes are big. Chickens cry out. Some dogs wail. Their eyes are wide with fear."

Ingrid's obsession with animals' feelings date back at least to age five, when she was on holiday in France with her mother and her father, a navigational engineer who was putting up radar stations throughout the south of France, in towns such as Perpignan and Carcassone. She remembers this as one of the happiest times of her life because her parents took her out of school in Cornwall in order for her to accompany them and because she could spend time with her father, who had often been away from home on business.

"I remember coming into these towns. We had enormous equipment with us, so my father had a convoy of trucks, and everybody would come out to see what was rumbling through the little town. It was like a parade and then we would go and have lunch with the mayor," she recalled.

On the trip, her father taught Ingrid the first French words she learned—how to say "please," "thank you," and "an ice cream, please, sir." Accompanying them was Seanie, the family's Irish setter. An only child, Ingrid felt Seanie was like a brother, but she had an affinity for all animals, playing with the chickens, cats, dogs, and guinea fowl, as well as the children, in the towns they visited.

One day, in the midst of this pleasant vacation, Ingrid walked around a corner of the bungalow her family was staying in, to find a man cutting off a chicken's head—a chicken she had played with earlier. "I was devastated," she said. "I had never thought about what people do to make a meal. It was hideously shocking to me. I remember crying and carrying on and my mother trying to comfort me."

Shortly afterward—she can't remember if it was the same day or a day later—her mother drove her into town. As little

Ingrid looked out the window, she saw a car crash into a woman on a motor scooter and watched the victim hit the pavement. "Of course these two events coming so close together had a horrific impact on me. And I said to myself, I'm not going to eat meat. That was my first stab at vegetarianism," said Ingrid. She succeeded for several days, because she stopped eating altogether. Then her mother, undoubtedly alarmed, gradually persuaded her to return to a "normal" diet. Still, Ingrid told me she felt troubled about eating meat. This letter is to her five-year-old self.

Dear Ingrid,

What you're feeling is the right thing to feel. You don't want to eat animals, and you shouldn't have to, because animals are your friends and you want to be a good friend to them.

Now you feel miserable after being so happy on your holiday. But you mustn't feel bad because you didn't stick to your plan. It's very hard for someone your age to change Mummy's mind. She believes she is doing the best thing for you.

Still, you are learning something important. You've listened to what's in your heart. If you think that you're going to do something hurtful—and you don't want to do it—you should say to someone who tries to make you, "Will you help me stick to my resolve? Will you not try, even if you have all the good intentions in the world, to shake my resolve? Don't fool me, persuade me, trick me, tempt me, or frighten me into forgetting that I have these feelings."

Years from now, when you're twenty-one, you will try again. You'll find out about the terrible lives that animals have on farms that are like factories, so you'll want to quit eating meat. A man

you are living with will tease you about becoming a vegetarian. And
he'll tempt you to change your mind by making wonderful-smelling
roast chicken.

When that happens, you'll know what to do. You'll sit him
down and say, "You're supposed to love me. So that means you're
supposed to help me. I'm not doing this because I don't like the taste
of animals. I'm making this decision, which is hard for me, because
I care about animals and I don't want to eat them anymore." And
you'll succeed.

With respect,
Ingrid

JANE BRYANT QUINN

Author and Columnist

"About your kids—it's okay."

THE TRUE TEST of personal finance advice, rarely administered, is how well it ages. Pick up a yellowed column on a past investment fad—dot-com stocks in the late 1990s, say, or real estate partnerships in the 1980s—and few writers' counsel looks as smart today as it sounded back then. Jane Bryant Quinn, a regular contributor to *Newsweek* and *Good Housekeeping,* is an exception. She began leveling straight talk at consumers long before investment chatter infiltrated every media outlet every hour of the day. She digs deeper than most journalists and cuts through hype like a surgeon.

Her knowledge is encyclopedic, as is reflected in her two giant best-selling tomes, *Making the Most of Your Money* and *Everybody's Money Book.* Among a long list of accolades, Jane has won the Gerald Loeb Award for Lifetime Achievement and for Distinguished Business and Financial Journalism and—three times—landed the National Press Club Award for Consumer Journalism. Her 2006 book, *Jane Bryant Quinn's Smart and Simple Money Strategies for Busy People,* explains how to keep your finances safely on track while you get on with the rest of your life.

When I worked with her at *Newsweek,* I learned that in person Jane is just as levelheaded and direct as her no-nonsense columns, but not as steadfastly serious. Quick with rejoinders, she's a witty conversationalist and sharp-eyed observer of the business scene. A lover of opera, symphonic music, and the theater, she recently bought an apartment in New York City after years of commuting from a northern Westchester suburb. Her letter, written to herself when her two sons were teenagers, is about navigating one of parenting's most treacherous passages.

Dear Jane,

About your kids—it's okay. They'll grow up. Teenagers are God's justice—your turn to feel the kind of heat you turned on your own parents at sixteen. Remember when your father threatened to shoot your boyfriend for unpublishable infractions? Remember the fights with your mother about your freedom and your hair? You were, of course, an angel compared with kids today, but still. . . .

You're at the point during your sons' teenage years when you've quit having expectations and begun to worry simply about keeping them alive. A litany is running through your head: Will they total the car? Do drugs? Sell drugs? Drop out of school? Run away? Punch out their father? Hate me for years? Hate me always?

Am I a bad parent? you ask yourself. Are they bad kids?

Hair and smoking are the least of it. You're wondering if your kids will ever get themselves together, end the drift, secure a job, find a life. You're searching to discover what you can do to keep them from falling off a cliff. You question if you'll ever forge a happy relationship again.

If you gave me a chance to turn back the clock to these parenting years, I wouldn't! Hold tight, because it's going to happen. Not right away—you'll discover that the teen years can extend well into the mid-twenties, with the same misunderstandings and fights. But your kids are going to get a life (of course they will!). Eventually, your fears will die down. Your sense of responsibility for them will ebb as you see them become responsible for themselves. You're doing your best as a parent, and next you'll be able to reclaim your own life and leave them to theirs.

In the future, you and your boys will talk about these years, and laugh (at least most of the time). You'll do some things wrong— worry too much, try too hard to control events, miss a couple of important issues that you'll wish you'd seen.

On the other hand, kids hide things and you can't read their devious, antiparent minds. And you're doing one thing right: In extremis, you chant to yourself, "I'm the grown-up, they're the kids." That helps you keep a little perspective during wilder moments.

As it will turn out, you'll raise happy, reliable men of good conscience and good character. Whew. Their way won't be your way, but that shouldn't surprise you. Once they grow up—and you relax—the family will come together again. Believe it or not, eventually the kids are going to feel responsible for you!

God's justice, again, although you and I haven't yet given them a very hard time. Hmm. Maybe we should take up smoking and tattoo our ear.

Love,
Jane

PHYLICIA RASHAD

Actress

"Put yourself, and your growth and development, first."

Pꜰʏʟɪᴄɪᴀ ʀᴀꜱʜᴀᴅ ɪꜱ an old soul. As Claire Huxtable, on *The Cosby Show*, she was supposed to be a high-powered attorney, but she always radiated a sense of extraordinary calm. Her high, pacific forehead looks incapable of furrowing in worry. Her soothing, low-pitched voice curls lovingly around each word that she utters. Here's a woman who seems permanently tapped into the universe's hum.

Phylicia's eight-year run on *The Cosby Show* obscured her considerable stage skills, so many were surprised to see her range when playing Lena in *A Raisin in the Sun,* for which she won a Tony in 2004. In fact, she was trained for the theater and has performed on Broadway in *The Wiz* and *Dreamgirls,* as well as in many Off-Broadway and regional theater productions, including *Everybody's Ruby, The Vagina Monologues,* and *Medea.* Phylicia credits her mother, a published poet and author, with giving her a sense of duty about exploring her potential.

That exploration began in earnest when she moved to New

York City to begin an acting career a few months after graduating from Howard University. As valuable as that time was, Phylicia says she wasn't particularly aware of the panorama of opportunities and experiences set before her when she began living in the city. "It's interesting how you wander through these things. Grace is always present and grace stands to shelter and guide and protect us. There comes a time in life when you really must become conscious of that presence and you must consciously turn your face to it. Otherwise, you're just walking blindly through life," she says, adding that this perspective has nothing to do with religion or religious beliefs.

This letter is to her twenty-one-year-old self, living at the Y in Manhattan and enjoying a widening circle of friends.

∽℮⌇

Dear Phylicia,

You are experiencing a time that won't come again—not like this. This is time to spend carefully and deliberately. Romantic involvement distracts you and can blind you to what's really in front of you. And what is really in front of you? You are. You don't even know yourself yet. You don't really know who you are. You think you know and you want to assert that you do—now that you're a certain age—but you don't. What is in front of you is a whole world of experiences beyond your imagination. Put yourself, and your growth and development, first.

There are long-term repercussions to what you're doing now. Every action you take, every thought you have, every word you say creates a memory that you will hold in your body. This is happening all the time. So this is the greater message: Every action creates a

memory that is imprinted upon you and affects you in subtle ways—
ways you are not always aware of.

   With that in mind, be very conscious and selective.

                              With high hopes for you,
                              Phylicia

ANN REINKING

Dancer and Choreographer

∽◌◡◌∽

"I promise you, this will pass."

ANN REINKING, FIFTY-SIX, has one of those bodies
that looks like it's all legs. So I asked. For the record, the
five-foot-six-and-a-half-inch choreographer and dancer meas-
ures forty-one and a half inches from waist to heel—62 percent of her height. That's about average. What accounts for
her immense presence in Broadway shows such as *Chicago,
Cabaret, Dancin'*, and *Fosse*? The enchantment of a true enter-
tainer. Think of Annie with one leg on the stage, the other
pointing heavenward in a 180-degree split, her head thrown
back and her thousand-megawatt smile suggesting that this
hamstring-fraying position is so much fun that she just may
hold it indefinitely.

One of seven children, she started dance lessons in sixth
grade, later winning a Ford Foundation scholarship to study
with the San Francisco School of Ballet and a scholarship to
study with Robert Joffrey. Her first job, right out of high
school, was with the Corps de Ballet at Radio City Music
Hall. She moved on to perform in Broadway shows, television

productions, and films. In 1997, she raked in a slew of awards, including the Tony, the Drama Desk, and the Astaire, for her choreography for the Encores! production of *Chicago*.

Still choreographing and directing theater productions, Ann is also the artistic adviser of the Broadway Theater Project, a program in Tampa, Florida, that exposes talented young performers to working professionals. "We want to create great dancers, in part, by creating great dancers' minds. We teach kids how to manage being a teenager and how to manage stress, because these are essential skills that aren't taught elsewhere," she says.

Dance, in fact, helped save Ann from a dismal nadir in her younger years. Her father's work as a traveling salesman uprooted the family every year or so. By the time Ann was eight or nine years old, she was a lonely girl and didn't have many friends in Fullerton, California, where her family lived. Though she found comfort with her family, she felt marooned between two sets of male siblings who preferred each other's company to hers. Her letter is to that quiet girl with a Peter Pan haircut who spent a lot of time alone in her room and in the pool at a local swim club.

Annie, my friend,

I'm with you there, floating and twirling underwater at Jimmy Smith's Swim Club, your refuge. There, we're free of school's hallway hierarchy—who's popular, who's not. The chlorine sea washes away the puzzle of kids who sometimes act mean and other times are nice. Let's slither through the obstacle course of lower-half bodies under the pool's surface.

*I'm with you. I know how distraught you feel, not being
accepted. Sometimes it's fine, it really is, and you feel at home. But
then other times, you feel so left out. When you try to be friendly,
you aren't very good at it. It doesn't come off right, and that makes
everything crummier.*

*You believe you're the only kid suffering like this—and that you
caused it. You don't know why, but it feels like you've been singled
out. And even though you talk to your mom about a lot of things,
you feel you have to bear this alone, to protect your parents from
knowing that their child is a misfit.*

*What presses most heavily on your heart is that this is a
permanent condition. This is how life will be for you, always.*

*Annie, relief is just around the corner. You're in a phase where
one year seems like ten, but I promise you, this will pass. Things will
change—and so much for the better. Your parents will want to settle
down, so they'll move the family to Seattle, the beautiful green city
where you stay in your grandmother's big brick Tudor during the
summers. You'll run on the mud flats at Nooshkum, one of the
most peaceful places on earth.*

*The move will restore you to such happiness and then—you'll
discover dance. Your body will start singing at this new use of it.
Your parents will let you put a barre in your room so you can
practice. Dance will lead you into the rest of your life like a
charging guardian angel.*

> *With kindness,*
> *Ann*

COKIE ROBERTS

Columnist and Commentator

"There's no need to be doing it all at once."

WE SHOULD ALL be as productive while multitasking as Cokie Roberts, a sixty-year-old political analyst for ABC and National Public Radio as well as a syndicated newspaper columnist. She spoke to me by phone from her basement office in Bethesda, Maryland, where several grandchildren played on the floor as she assembled the footnotes for her new book. Her career is studded with accolades, including the Edward R. Murrow Award and an Emmy. She's written three books, two of which have been best-sellers: *We Are Our Mother's Daughters* and *From This Day Forward*.

These days, working while tending to toddlers is old hat. But when Cokie became a mother, it was almost unheard of. Her son, Lee, arrived when Cokie was twenty-four, and Rebecca when she was twenty-six. "To show you how different an era it was, we didn't have even one second of conversation about me leaving my job. We both assumed I would leave. But I thought it was important for me to continue to work for my own sanity and because I thought it was expected of an educated person," she explained. Cokie continued writing and working in television, mostly from home, after her kids were born.

Cokie remembers those years as baby mayhem. "We didn't have money. We didn't have help. Steve was away a lot," she recalled. "I say all of this by way of description—not by way of saying it was a hard life. I've been around people who've led really hard lives." Still, the day-in, day-out drudgery often made her feel trapped and muffled. Here's what she would like to say to herself as a young mother.

༄

Dear Cokie,

Is this a life sentence? Will you spend the rest of your life with jelly stains on your knees? Will your kids ever sleep through the night?

Being the mother of two tiny kids frazzles you because the utterly banal is, somehow, profoundly important. Nothing could be more mindless than wiping noses and pouring apple juice—yet you know there's no bigger job. For so much to hinge on so little is brain-numbing. It's as if world peace depended on how well you dust your living room. Worse, you were never any good at homemaking arts, apart from cooking. Now you're supposed to put toys away and clean out the tub as if your children's entire future success hangs in the balance?

This kind of absurd mismatch between day-to-day motherhood and the emotional charge it carries can be a little scary. Your kids, like all kids, are a pain in the neck sometimes. As a regular person in your regular life, you really don't get angry. But as a mother, you're shocked at your capacity for anger with your children.

Instead of childish misbehavior, their transgressions seem like terrible reflections on you as a mother.

Here's my advice about the anger, chaos, and isolation. First, beware the dangers of extrapolation in motherhood. Despite his impressive tantrums, your willful son will not throw himself on the floor of grocery stores, screaming for candy, when he's grown up. Just because your daughter can't seem to stop talking now doesn't mean she won't ever. Also, understand that this won't last forever. Don't feel oppressed by it. These are very short years in the scheme of life and you will live through them.

You're trying to fit everything in at once, working for a TV station and a magazine. But Cokie, you'll be in the workplace for fifty years, literally. There's no need to be doing it all at once. At times you do have to, but there are times when you don't. You can leave the work world—and come back on your own terms.

One more thing: There will be compensation! Your children will grow up to be charming and caring people—who will produce adorable grandchildren. Your willful son will someday have an extremely willful daughter. One of your daughter's sons will talk incessantly. And guess who will have patience for all of that and more? You.

Hang in there.

Love,
Cokie

NORA ROBERTS

Author

"Laundry will wait very patiently."

A HOME'S MOST IMPORTANT rule speaks volumes about life there. In Nora Roberts's house, the rule for her sons, Dan and Jason, was that they could not interrupt their mother when she was working unless there was blood or fire. A single mom of two little boys who wrote at home without a baby-sitter, she felt the opposing, inescapable pulls of work and motherhood daily in the late 1970s and early 1980s. "When they got older, the rule changed. I said, 'Okay, now it has to be arterial blood and active fire, because you're old enough to handle these things,' " she says.

Nora's time-management system obviously worked. Her sons, Dan, thirty-three, and Jason, thirty, grew up happy and healthy. She has written more than 160 novels, 125 of them best-sellers, including fourteen written as J. D. Robb. In those early days, though, success seemed far away. Writing was the second income-producing activity she tried, after being a "really bad legal secretary," she says. Publishers rejected several manuscripts—three years' worth of writing—before her first novel, *Irish Thoroughbred,* was published in 1981. In this letter, Nora, fifty-five, writes to herself at thirty-one, as her writing career began to gather steam.

Dear Nora,

Being a mother is the number-one priority for you, no question. But you're also the sole source of your little family's income. So you've been driving yourself hard, writing at home with the kids underfoot. It's terribly intense. Your boys fight constantly, as boys do. The oldest one's mission in life apparently is to destroy his younger brother. You wonder, Are they going to hate each other for life? Am I raising psychopaths?

Sometimes—well, often—it's chaos, with laundry piling up and toys strewn everywhere. How am I going to get through this? *you ask yourself.*

Nora, you're actually doing a pretty good job. Some days you don't do so well, I admit. But other days you do. My advice: When juggling as much as you are, remember that some balls are glass and some are rubber. You can't drop the glass balls. Also, learn to put on blinders about certain things. Laundry will wait very patiently.

Remember the day you were supposed to appear on Good Morning America *and Jason, evading a girl who was trying to kiss him, ran smack into a flagpole? You picked him up, took him to get three stitches, and got blood all over your white jacket. You missed an incredible opportunity to get word out about your book, but that was the right choice about a glass ball.*

The next time you start to torture yourself about what kind of mother you are, think of this. When Dan is twenty-two—which, believe it or not, he will be one day—he'll move into his own apartment. *The day he moves, he'll send you flowers with a note that says, "Thanks for always being there." That's the kind of son you're raising.*

One more thing. Pressed from all corners, you often think, If I could just have eight hours of quiet. *You will have that someday, but you won't have those little guys you have now and you'll miss them.*

With love,
Nora

"Relax and enjoy your success."

J OYCE ROCHÉ, FIFTY-NINE, president and chief executive officer of Girls Inc., a not-for-profit organization in
New York City, grew up one of eleven kids in a low-income
African-American family in New Orleans. Feminism and the
civil rights movement were fast changing the world for young
black women when she entered college in 1967, but not so
quickly that Joyce lifted her sights beyond the goal of becoming a teacher. That was aiming high, by her family's standards.
She was only the second in her family to attend college. Then
in 1969, during her senior year at Dillard University in New
Orleans, Joyce dated a man who had gone to business school.

"I had never even thought of going to graduate school—and
definitely not thought about business. But I knew that I needed
to open my lens. So I applied to Columbia and got in," she says.
That heady moment was the beginning of a decade of jumping
at unfamiliar opportunities that felt like wild gambles at the
time but then paid off with bigger opportunities. She joined
Avon after business school in 1973 and worked like a demon.

Promoted almost yearly for the first five years, she constantly faced new job challenges. Then in 1979, she was recruited to join Revlon to be director of marketing. Determined to prove herself in a dog-eat-dog work environment, Joyce redoubled her already punishing work habits. Success at Revlon prompted Avon to lure her back with the promise of becoming an officer of the company, the first African-American woman to do so.

After nineteen years at Avon, Joyce was vice president of global marketing and had held every marketing job at the company. Looking for general management experience, she became president and chief operating officer of Carson Products Co., an African-American personal-care company in Savannah, Georgia (it has since been purchased by L'Oréal). Six years ago, she stepped into her current post. Girls Inc. reaches some 500,000 girls each year with programming that has been proven to be effective in the organization's research laboratory.

Its motto: Inspiring All Girls to Be Strong, Smart, and Bold. Acting that way came naturally to Joyce. But inner confidence didn't. Here she writes to herself at age thirty-four, toward the end of her term at Revlon.

Dear Joyce,

You never set out to be a pioneer, but here you are, out front, one of the few African-American women dancing up the corporate ladder. You achieve more every year, but each leap exerts more pressure. Who would have thought success could feel so much like a burden?

You clearly thrive on it. You love marketing, and the more you work, the more you're consumed and fascinated by it. Here at Revlon, you're setting a personal record, working from 8:00 or so in the morning until 9:30 or 10:00 at night—and both days on the weekend. Exercise? Forget about it. You can't even plan a lunch because chances are that a meeting will be called at noon.

You're not complaining, because, strangely, there's a giddiness in such hard work. You risked a lot when you seized every opportunity that presented itself. Laboring ever more intensely shows you're worthy of the chances you've been given. It also props open the door for every African-American woman who might be coming behind you.

This is what you tell yourself—and it's all true. But it only goes so far. The way you drink up that steady stream of praise and recognition is a tip-off. You did a good job. You belong here. We want to make you an officer of the company.

Ever wonder why the glow wears off so soon? Because somewhere, deep inside, you don't believe what they say. You think it's a matter of time before you stumble and "they" discover the truth. You're not supposed to be here. We knew you couldn't do it. We should never have taken a chance on you.

The threat of failure scares you into these long hours. Yet success only intensifies the fear of discovery.

Stop. It. Now. You're not an imposter. You're the genuine article. You have the brainpower. You have the ability. You don't have to work so hard and worry so much. You're going to do just fine. You deserve a place at the table.

So relax and enjoy your success.

Love,
Joyce

LISA SCOTTOLINE

Novelist

∞

"The way you look matters far less than you think."

BEFORE SHE BECAME a best-selling mystery writer, Lisa Scottoline was on a fast-track legal career. Born and raised in Philadelphia, she attended the University of Pennsylvania, where she made time to help establish the Penn Women's Row Team while cramming four years of credits into three. After graduating magna cum laude, she went to Penn's law school, married, and landed a prestigious clerkship for a state appellate judge in 1981.

A demanding job as a litigator at Dechert, Price & Rhoads followed. By the time she was pregnant with her daughter, five years later, however, her marriage was failing. It ended shortly after her daughter was born, leaving Lisa, who wanted to stay at home with her baby, in a bind. A devotee of Grisham and Turow books, she speculated that readers might have an appetite for legal thrillers written by a woman. Much to the consternation of her parents, the spunky thirty-year-old decided to give herself five years or fifty thousand dollars in debt—whichever came first—to write and sell her first novel.

Five years later, she had five maxed-out credit cards and a completed novel, *Everywhere That Mary Went*. The book sold to HarperCollins a week after Lisa began a part-time job clerking for a judge, and it was nominated for the Edgar Award by the Mystery Writers of America. Lisa, now fifty, has written twelve books, including the *New York Times* best-sellers *Mistaken Identity* and *Moment of Truth*. Her latest, published in March 2006, is *Dirty Blonde*. Though her unusual career path took guts to pursue, Lisa's list of essential knowledge for herself at age twenty-five shows that she wasn't always so confident.

Dear Lisa,

   Here are the ten things you need to know.

1. *Your hair matters far, far less than you think.*
2. *In fact, the way you look matters far less than you think.*
3. *"Can I ask a dumb question?" is never a good thing to say.*
4. *In fact, asking permission to speak is never a good idea at all.*
5. *While we're on the subject, don't speak too fast because you're afraid of wasting your listener's time. Listening to what you have to say is the highest and best use of anyone's time. Even if your hair looks terrible.*
6. *And don't edit what you say before you say it. That would be you, getting in the way of truth, and, worse, of your heart.*
7. *You are already working approximately 25 percent harder than you have to to get the result you want. Chillax.*

8. *Don't hang out with anyone who doesn't understand why you're so wonderful, or who needs to be told, or who doesn't tell you at regular intervals or when you forget.*

9. *That little voice you keep ignoring is the only one you should ever listen to.*

10. *Love.*

Lisa

BEVERLY SILLS

Opera Singer

"Be glad for every moment."

BEVERLY SILLS'S MOTHER insisted that her daughter, born Belle Silverman and nicknamed "Bubbles," would be an opera singer from the time she was a baby. When the little girl was two, her aunt Rose asked Beverly's mother what she would do if the diva in the making didn't have a voice. "*My* daughter will have a voice," her mother said with quiet vehemence. Beverly Sills, a coloratura soprano who reigned as one of the New York City Opera and Metropolitan Opera's foremost stars, is still bemused by her mother's self-assurance. "My family is a dynasty of doctors. There's not a musician in the bunch," she says. "It was almost as if she willed it."

Beverly spoke with me in her office at Lincoln Center, where she had pulled off a highly unusual second act after retiring from singing in 1980. As general director of the New York City Opera, she turned around the financially unstable company and converted it into a self-sustaining company. She went on to become chairwoman of Lincoln Center for the Performing Arts from 1994 to 2002, and chairwoman of the

Metropolitan Opera until 2005. She was especially pleased on the day I saw her, because a donor had made a large gift to ensure that the Met's radio broadcasts could continue.

Influential as her mother was, it's her father Beverly writes about in her letter. A five-pack-a-day smoker, he died of lung cancer when she was twenty. "He spoke with huge periods at the end of every sentence. For me, he was my Rock of Gibraltar, because there was never any doubt about what he expected—what would disappoint him and what was a real no-no. There was a right and a wrong and there was never any question about what was in his mind," she recalled.

When Beverly was ten, she had started her singing lessons and told her father that she wanted to be onstage. He informed her that only hussies go on the stage. "Papa, what's a hussy?" she asked. His response: "A woman who wears low-cut dresses, too much makeup, and changes the color of her hair." "So, of course, I was instantly hooked on the idea," she said with a laugh. Here, Beverly, in her seventies, writes to herself at sixteen, after her father traveled to Detroit and first saw her sing onstage, in *The Merry Widow.*

Dear Bubbles,

Your father forbade you to go on tour. He said that if you did, you could not come home. The only reason you're performing on tour with J. J. Shubert is because Mother insisted that you be allowed to go—and she told your father that you could come home to her half of the house.

But then she persuaded him to travel all the way to Detroit to see you last night. You didn't know he was in the audience, so when he knocked on your door at the end of the performance, you were surprised to see him. He looked you up and down. There you were in a low-cut dress, with tons of stage makeup and a different hair color.

"See, you look terrible," he said.

Oh God, you thought, this is the end.

Then he gave you the most wonderful review you will ever get, from the most knowledgeable critic you'll probably ever have. He said, "You sing like an angel. Come home. I'll pay for your lessons."

He's tall, dark, curly-haired, and very handsome. You know him as a strict father with high expectations, but he loves you so. You won't have him to love back for as long as you should. So, Beverly, talk as much as you can to this well-read man. He won't get to see how well his lessons on behavior, dress, and right and wrong will serve you—nor how accomplished you'll become. But you'll be glad for every moment you spend with him now.

Love,
Beverly

LIZ SMITH

Gossip Columnist

$\sim\!\mathcal{Q}\!\sim$

*"It's not psychologically good for you
to make yourself a little person."*

A T EIGHTY-THREE, Liz Smith, a television commentator and syndicated gossip columnist at the *Daily News,
Newsday,* and the *New York Post* for decades, has a few modest
regrets. She wishes she had made more of her college education and less of the opportunities for fun at the University of
Texas at the end of World War II. She's sorry she didn't keep
a better record of her activities—including photos, names, and
dates. "You should live as though you know you are going to
be famous. Even if you aren't, you'll still have the satisfaction
of knowing exactly how you spent your time," she says. But
all in all, she is finding old age to be very agreeable. "I'm a lot
happier than I used to be. I was so riddled with ambition and
I thought I was such a hot shit in my younger years," she says,
ever frank.

Driven to make a name for herself when she landed in
New York in 1949 with a fifty-dollar grubstake, she became a
small-time reporter, typist, and proofreader. Eventually, she

landed "important jobs working for dynamic men in that era, before women's liberation," she says. Among them were Mike Wallace at CBS Radio and Allen Funt on *Candid Camera*.

In her zeal to succeed and impress, she made a fundamental career error in some of those early years. Here she writes to herself in her early thirties, when she began working for Norman Frank, a producer at NBC.

❧

Dear Liz,

You're an extremely hard worker, and enterprising to boot. In the long run, these attributes will bring you the success you want.

But right now, Liz, you're using those terrific traits in a negative way. When you're asked to research a segment, scout a location, or do any one of the hundreds of other tasks that go into producing Dave Garroway's Wide Wide World, *you diligently unearth every relevant detail. But you take special, secret pleasure when your diligence produces some kind of obstacle to your boss's plan. You love saying to this powerful, successful man, "I've researched it to the max and it's not possible to do."*

It's human nature, when you're underpaid and working too hard, while these people over you are famous and rich. The impulse is to thumb your nose at them.

You must wake up to what you're doing, however. It's not psychologically good for you to make yourself a little person. You have to rise above that impulse. Instead of "laying dead kittens at their feet," saying, "No, it can't be done," you must become part of the solution.

You may feel that you'll never achieve what these powerful bosses have, but you may be taken aback at what happens when you begin to make your bosses' problems your own problems to solve. Give it all you've got. Drop the envy and secret malice.

Go get 'em, tiger.

Liz

PICABO STREET

Olympic Skier

"Chill out, ride the gravy train, and have fun."

THE FEROCIOUS WILL that led skier Picabo Street past knee injuries, concussions, broken bones, and mangled ligaments to numerous World Cup victories, a silver in the 1994 Olympics at Lillehammer, a gold in the 1998 Olympics in Nagano, and a last hurrah at the 2002 Olympics in Salt Lake City, is not all that remarkable, according to Picabo. Flying down a mountain at ninety miles an hour was simply what was normal to her. So whenever an injury derailed her, her focus on recovery narrowed to laser-beam dimensions.

"Imagine not being able to do something that's as normal as breathing to you. You have to regain that ability, to get back to where you were, so that you can move on. It's just that the realm of what I used to do is different from yours. My gauge is a little different," she explains.

Now thirty-five, living in Park City, Utah, and married to John Mulligan, Picabo's gauge has been radically recalibrated by the birth of her son Treyjan, named after a powerful Roman emperor. "At this moment my rewards are little things.

Watching a movie. Taking a bath. Making it through the day with Trey—without him having a gas attack!"

She wishes she could have had some of this equanimity earlier—particularly after she won the gold medal in 1998. Immediately after the momentous event, she took an eleven-day vacation in Hawaii with her family, boyfriend, and friends, and then hurried to Switzerland to participate in World Cup races. There, on Friday the thirteenth, in March, she crashed, breaking her left leg and blowing out her right knee. "I was off skis for one year and nine months and change. It was a long time and it was difficult. I was frustrated and lost. I wasn't done skiing, so couldn't move on," says Picabo.

It's a chapter in her life that she would redo if she could. Her letter is written to herself just after she won the gold in the Super G, at age twenty-seven.

◦◦◦

Dear Picabo,

Who could know that having won an Olympic gold medal—your lifetime dream since age eleven—would be harder than trying to win it?

You're so surprised and shocked and satisfied and relieved that you won, but it makes you feel lost, in no-man's-land. You feel like you've been on a train going three hundred miles an hour and then it stops. You were in a full-tilt boogie toward that dream of your life. All of a sudden—boom!—it happened.

You don't really realize what's going on yet. So I'll tell you: Reaching your ultimate goal is a complete novelty. Rather than feeling satisfaction, you're feeling that it's all over, thinking, Nothing will be better than winning the gold medal.

Nothing will top this. *Being removed from that medium of striving, constant striving, is taking your compass away.*

Athletes have a hard time shifting into neutral. Idle time isn't good for people who are driven. Even so, I'm going to give you some advice that will be hard to follow. Your boyfriend is telling you to chill out, ride the gravy train, and have fun.

I say do it.

Go home, go to Los Angeles, go to New York. Do all the talk shows and the parties and make yourself available to corporate America. It will be scary, because this is unknown territory. Being satisfied, letting yourself be patted on the back—that's unnatural as hell. And very uncomfortable for you. It's easier to be on the warpath. You don't even like champagne.

You want to go to the World Cup races in Crans-Montana, Switzerland. You're thinking, The only way to top a gold medal is to win two. *But that's because you don't know how to enjoy your achievement. Switzerland will be disastrous for you. You're going to have to learn how to pat yourself on the back eventually. Start now. It's not gloating. It's taking pleasure in life's goodness.*

You've always been a speed junkie, but it's time to understand that slowing down has its rewards, too.

> *Your shadow on the mountain,*
> *P.*

JOYCE TENNESON

Photographer

∽◉◞

"Your best work will come in moments of grace."

I T ' S   H U M B L I N G   T O   try to describe the creations of photographer Joyce Tenneson. Her images are so filled with
emotion that words seem too vacant for the task. Still, the arc
of her work, documented in ten books and over two hundred
shows, is what you must track to understand Joyce. "I felt my
destiny was to be an artist—to somehow use my personal journey as my artwork. And that's really what I've done over the
last thirty years, to really record the different chapters in my
life visually," she says.

Moving backward, then, consider some images from the
thousands she has generated. In *Intimacy,* a book of flower por-
traiture published by Barnes & Noble in 2004, two white or-
chids float, stemless, on a pure black background. One flower,
in the distance, has four petals, each with its own agenda. A
second flower fills the foreground, but we see only its top
half—petals that look like a beckoning finger and a headdress.
Alone, each orchid is beautiful. But together, the beckoning
fingers curving toward one another, they make a private con-

versation, or a dance, between flowers that we've never witnessed.

This sharp intimacy reflects Joyce now, at sixty, after breaking through years of chrysalis. "I feel like I've been struggling all my life, just to be validated as an artist," she says. In *Transformations,* Joyce's sense of being bound, of needing to tear open the chrysalis's shroud, was movingly portrayed by figures wrapped in or covered by sheer netting. "I've always been interested in the world that we can't see," Joyce says.

She grew up on the grounds of a convent near Boston, one of four children close in age. Her mother was a twin, and her connection with this sister, who often lived with Joyce's family, seemed deeper than her relationship with her husband or her children. Joyce married when she was "twenty, going on ten, to get out of the house, because nice Catholic girls didn't live with men back then," she explains. Though she always felt she had a gift, holding fast to an artist's identity in her late twenties proved daunting.

"My family never encouraged this. I never had a mentor. I never had a role model. It was something very fierce and deep within myself," she says. Living in Washington, D.C., the mother of a young child and wife of a scientist, Joyce felt isolated from other artists. She made thousands of self-portraits in her twenties—along with teaching photography, getting her master's degree at night, mothering a young son, and writing a book—as a way to explore who she really was amid the welter of roles she was playing. A bookend to these question-marked self-portraits is the best-selling *Wise Women* she authored twenty-eight years later, which features the sharply delineated personalities of ninety women, ages sixty-five to one hundred. Here is Joyce's letter to the lonely, trapped young artist she once was.

Dear Joyce,

Every day you're marking out your vision, like a surveyor, trying to do work that is deeply personal and comes from your heart. You believe, like Jung, that what's most profoundly personal is also most universal. But it's a daily struggle to stay true to yourself, because right now the art world won't acknowledge—much less praise—art with female energy.

You're not trying to do female art, with a capital F, but your vision is authentic to you. And that's just not being well received by the major art power brokers. You wonder if you're deluding yourself by being persistent, clinging to the direction your inner map dictates. Maybe there's something I'm not seeing, *you think.* Maybe my fundamental instinct is off.

Let me answer those doubts. You are completely on the right track. You will not be sorry about your path. And though critical praise will come, another form of validation, which will be even more meaningful, will reach you. After your eighth book, you will get letters from all over the world from people who have seen your work. They'll thank you. They'll tell you how you've changed their lives. This will feel like being bathed in love—your work reaching out like a giant oar to stir the insides of complete strangers. This will be an unexpected benediction, more resounding and satisfying than you could have expected.

It's all ahead of you, true, decades ahead. But try to feel that invisible audience with you, even now, watching, appreciating the currents your steadfast little heart is navigating. They're out there.

I know how hard it is to make this journey without fellow artists or words of encouragement. When you lie in your bed at night and read Virginia Woolf or Anaïs Nin to shore yourself up, understand that you are such a brave and courageous person—and a beautiful person. I know you don't feel that way, but that's because you're very tough on yourself, Joyce. A family habit, isn't it? None of you were ever good enough growing up.

In fact, you're being incredibly honorable by staying in Washington, D.C., despite the toll on your life as an artist. You believe that moving to New York would put your son's emotional well-being in jeopardy. So you're waiting. It will take a long time to circle back to you, but the goodness in that choice will return, amplified, both in your work and your son.

This is the decade when you're being sternly schooled in waiting and being true to yourself. What you'll discover is that your best work will come in moments of grace. You can't will those into being. But if you stay true to yourself, hone your craft—and wait— they will appear magically from time to time.

> Carry on, my friend,
> Joyce

VANNA WHITE

Wheel of Fortune Hostess

"Always follow your heart."

W HEN VANNA BECAME a national obsession in the 1980s, she was one of the few one-named celebrities, along with Garbo, Cher, and Barbie. As Pat Sajak, *Wheel of Fortune*'s host, noted in the foreword of *Vanna Speaks,* Vanna's 1987 autobiography, "Her face has adorned more magazine covers than the universal pricing code."

Merv Griffin hired Vanna White for the *Wheel of Fortune* gig in December of 1982, after she had spent two years cobbling together modeling assignments and odd jobs in Los Angeles. The television show had been successful, but when it debuted in syndication in late 1983, suddenly the glamorous letter-turner became a sensation. Vanna, who only a short time earlier had often been hard-pressed to pay her rent, adored her job and fulfilled Americans' fantasies beautifully. She looked like a bombshell but had the apple-pie personality of the small-town southern girl that she is.

Just when Vanna mania seemed to be everywhere, disaster struck in 1986. A photographer who five years earlier had photographed Vanna in sexy lingerie for an advertisement now sold his pictures to *Playboy*. Vanna, who with her boyfriend had often been a guest of Hugh Hefner's at the Playboy Mansion, asked Hefner not to publish the photos. "I said, 'Please help me out here. This could ruin what I've worked for my whole life,' " she remembers. According to Vanna, Hef, as she called him, agreed to keep the photos out of the magazine, but he later told her the decision was out of his hands.

When the photographs appeared, Vanna thought her career was over. "It was devastating to me," she recalls. With the support of the *Wheel* producers, who knew the photos existed when they hired her, Vanna decided to address the mistake publicly on talk shows and appearances. "I was completely honest with America. This was a great lesson to be learned. I said, 'I posed for these shots. I really knew I shouldn't have, but I did it anyways. I'm sorry and I hope I have your support.' "

America forgave her, of course. Vanna hasn't spoken to Hefner since. Now forty-nine and the mother of eleven-year-old Nico and eight-year-old Giovanna, Vanna's letter is written to her twenty-four-year-old, pre-*Wheel* self.

ᴄ⁀

Dear Vanna Banana,

I know you're doing everything you can to make it in Los Angeles, which means paying that one-thousand-dollar rent every month without having to write home to ask Daddy for money. It's so important to you that he thinks everything is going just fine out there. When cash is tight, you occasionally take a waitress job to make ends meet. You've made it all work, but now you're really strapped. Eviction is right around the corner unless you find a way to make some money.

Please, though, don't pose for that lingerie ad. It means a lot of money—more than any modeling job has paid since you arrived in L.A. But there's something not quite right about it. You won't be posing nude, but the lingerie is not your basic Sears catalog underwear. It's sheer, only available through mail order.

It's only a lingerie ad. You figure no one will ever see it. But if you go forward with this, you'll be terribly uncomfortable revealing your body that way—so uncomfortable that you'll ask the photographer to conduct the shoot at your apartment. Even so, with every shot that he takes, you're going to think you shouldn't be doing it.

Listen to that little voice that is saying no. Call Daddy for a short-term loan. Some mistakes come back to bite you long after you've made them, and this one could bring down your career— where you will have more at stake than you could hope for.

Always follow your heart. If something feels wrong, it probably is.

With understanding,
Vanna

WENDY WALKER WHITWORTH

Producer of *Larry King Live*

∾⟨⟩⤳

*"Not getting pregnant will be the best thing
that ever happens to you. "*

WENDY WALKER WHITWORTH is one of those invisible forces who shapes our view of the world. As executive vice president of CNN and senior executive producer of Emmy-winning *Larry King Live* for the last thirteen years, she routinely lands exclusive interviews with newsmakers from every corner of celebrity land, including Nancy Reagan, Donald Trump, Martha Stewart, the late John F. Kennedy, Jr., Oprah Winfrey, and every living U.S. president. Apart from her stellar celebrity-wrangling skills, Wendy has brought a broad scope to *Larry King Live,* heightening the impact of what might have been a limited talk-show format. In 1995, for example, the show portrayed the Middle East peace process through interviews with PLO Chairman Yasser Arafat, King Hussein of Jordan, and Israeli Prime Minister Yitzhak Rabin. During the 2003 war in Iraq, Wendy produced live shows for twenty-nine consecutive days. Three generations of the Bush family gathered to talk on *Larry King Live* during the 2004 Republican National Convention.

You'd expect someone who has lived and breathed television news for more than twenty-five years—she was part of CNN when it debuted in 1980—to be a hard-edged neurotic with the attention span of a pinball. So it was a surprise to find a soft-voiced, undistracted blonde with arresting blue eyes when I walked into Wendy's office at CNN in New York, where she was crafting *Nancy Grace,* CNN's new legal-analysis show. Despite a heavy schedule, Wendy, wearing a glamorous black Valentino sweater-jacket and formidable stilettos, was unhurried and open.

Wendy never envisioned a working life. After growing up in Iowa and graduating from Hollins College, she was supposed to get married. "But that didn't happen," she explained. So, in 1975, she set out with four friends and a forty-dollar grubstake from her father to find a job in Washington, D.C. In a stint at Brooks Brothers, where she was a top-selling clerk, she discovered her competitive streak. While working as Ethel Kennedy's personal secretary, she helped with a televised celebrity tennis tournament and found her direction: television production. Speaking of herself at twenty-four, she said, "I thought, Well, my life is half over. I'm making this career decision at a very late age." But she forged ahead.

After landing the second job she applied for at ABC in Washington, she started work on the same day as Katie Couric, who became a good friend. Wendy logged videotapes, worked on Sundays, and pitched in wherever she was needed at ABC. Then her boss, George Watson, recruited her to join him in a move to CNN, a new channel, which proposed to produce twenty-four hours of news a day. For the next thirteen years, she roamed the White House, and then the globe, as once-scorned CNN gradually gained the respect of its peers. She joined *Larry King Live* in 1993.

Married just before she turned forty, Wendy was eager to start a family. When she failed to get pregnant, she embarked on the agonizing process of having a child through in vitro fertilization at forty-one. Her letter is written to herself at this stage, before her children, Amaya, now ten, and Walker, eight, entered her life.

Dear Wendy,

I know this has been a difficult few years for you. I am sure you thought that since your body seemed so fit and young on the outside, everything on the inside was going to work, too. And I know the disappointment you feel every time you find out it hasn't worked. I know how you always just expected to get pregnant. You never thought if, you only thought when. I know you wanted to run home and say those two words: "I'm pregnant."

You wanted to watch your stomach grow and laugh about the foods that made you sick and those you just craved and had to go out and get at 11:30 at night. You wanted to rush to the hospital and have your baby placed on your chest. You wanted to cry with joy and love for a little creature that was yours. And right now, that doesn't look like it is going to happen, does it?

I saw your sadness at Christmas when it didn't happen. And I heard your heart break when your sweet doctor called again with the news that it is unlikely you will carry a child. I remember the night you finally said you could not go through the process again, and I know you felt so alone.

I want to take this pain away for you. I hate to see you so sad.

I want to tell you that not getting pregnant will be the best thing that ever happens to you. It is a profound gift from the best energy in the universe. The stars will line up perfectly to bring you your gifts.

You will receive two amazing children, a boy and a girl. You will be with your daughter when she is born. She will be as beautiful inside as she is out. All the nurses will say she is the most beautiful baby they have ever seen. She will laugh like you and pout like you. She will have the spirit of an angel and the gentleness of a colt. Everyone will love her because her heart is so pure. She will be kind to everyone and you will not hear an unkind word spoken about her.

She will be embarrassed when you dance in the car while driving her to school and she will come to you when she has a private question. You will be so happy you didn't get pregnant. Because this child will fill your life so full of love that you will thank God every day that somehow it was just meant to be. She was meant to be yours.

And then you will be brought another little soul, this time a boy. You will be with him, too, when he is born. He will look just like you. And he will cling to you. He will not stop running. In fact, he will go from crawling to running. He will never walk. He will make you laugh every day and people will stop you on the street to talk to him. He will be a puzzle you will spend hours trying to put together. He will entertain you, challenge you, and be such a joy in your life. You will listen to his stories about dinosaurs over and over again. You will sing him to sleep while he has both arms around you.

There is a beautiful saying about adopted children, which is that they don't come from your stomach; they come from your heart. He is your heart. You will love him with everything you have and you will forget the pain you have now. Because you will thank God every day that somehow it was just meant to be. He was meant to be yours.

You won't even remember this time in your life very much because it will be so overcome by happiness with these children. This is happening to you for a reason. You will forever be grateful that you didn't get pregnant, because if you had, you would not have them. And they are your loves and your spirit. So tonight, go to sleep and dream about these two babies and soon they will be in your arms. The angels will bring them to you. It was meant to be. I promise.

Love,
Wendy

NAOMI   WOLF

Author

"Stop worrying about making people happy."

A TWENTY-SIX-YEAR-OLD Rhodes scholar, Naomi Wolf
was the bright, hard edge of feminism when her best-
selling *The Beauty Myth: How Images of Beauty Are Used Against
Women* was published in 1991. The book sparked great debate
and generated lots of attention for the beautiful and fierce
young woman. Naomi moved deeper into feminism's new
frontiers with *Fire with Fire: The New Female Power and How
It Will Change the 21st Century* in 1993. In that book, a different Naomi emerged. She describes the peculiarly feminine
downside of the success she had experienced.

> My self image was upended. I had always thought of my-
> self as warm, friendly, and feminine, for that was the re-
> action I had generally been able to count upon in close
> personal relationships. I did not recognize the person
> who was being reacted to as a critic, an antagonist, a
> threat to comfortable ideas—even though a critic was
> precisely what I had set out to be. . . . It got so that after
> a vigorous debate, I would come home and cry in my

partner's arms. . . . Then a lesser dragon, the Fear of Having Too Much, appeared in my life. . . . I reacted by moving further into the elaborate complex of stupidity about money that I had begun to pick up in college. Like many women, I went into a numbers-induced fog that enveloped me whenever I had to discuss my income. I was embarrassed talking to the woman who helped me with my taxes. I thought it was inappropriate for me to learn the least detail about handling my income.

In the following letter, forty-four-year-old Naomi, whose most recent book is *The Treehouse: Eccentric Wisdom from My Father on How to Live, Love and See*, offers practical advice to her cerebral twenty-eight-year-old self.

Dear Younger Self,

INVEST FIFTY BUCKS IN THE STOCK MARKET EVERY MONTH!! You don't need to eat out so much. Think of all that compound interest!

If they don't have beards and aren't clean-shaven either, they make good short-term but bad long-term boyfriends. Beware.

Stop worrying about making people happy or getting people's approval.

Forget trends; go for the classics.

Don't gossip; it makes you untrustworthy.

Condoms, condoms, condoms.

Kindness is everything.

Naomi Wolf

LEE ANN WOMACK

Singer and Songwriter

"Enjoy the moment, not the end result."

THE MESSAGE LEE Ann Womack, thirty-nine, wanted to send to herself was clear in one of the first comments out of her mouth: "There's so much about the last eight years, when all my dreams were coming true, that I don't remember," she said when we talked. On her way home to Nashville, where she lives with her husband, Frank Liddell, and two daughters, Aubrie, fifteen, and Ann Lise, seven, after performing in Utah, Lee Ann said that she had yearned for the kind of success she has now from the time she was a little girl growing up in Jacksonville, Texas. The only reason she went to Belmont University was that it was in Nashville. Though she enrolled in its music program, she had no serious plans to use her degree and never graduated.

Instead, she dreamed of touring with country-music star George Strait, being named CMA Female Vocalist of the Year, and putting out platinum albums. She thought her chances of achieving those goals were slim, but she did accomplish them, collecting numerous other awards, including a Grammy, as well. "Looking back now, I realize there were no limits," she says. Her most recent studio album, *There's More Where That Came From*, released in 2005, triggered another raft of CMA nominations: Album of the Year, Female Vocalist of the year, and Single and Music Video of the Year for "I May Hate Myself in the Morning."

Still, Womack's single-minded focus in the early years had a price. She had never even considered plan B—what she would fall back on if she didn't make it in the music world. For a while, nothing else in life seemed to matter except making herself a success. She describes what she lost as a result of that single-minded focus in a letter to herself at twenty-nine, when she was in the studio every day recording her first album, *Lee Ann Womack*.

Dear Lu,

You're a nervous wreck making this album. Your face is a mask of seriousness. You're walking around with a headache all the time. You can't tolerate much joking from the musicians and the engineer.

You're afraid that:

You'll do something wrong.

The songs might offend somebody.

The songs won't appeal to enough people.

The songs won't work on the radio.

You'll get up to bat and strike out.

Instead, cut the songs that you like and have fun doing it. Make a record that you enjoy, instead of making a record that you think will be successful.

You are so focused, uptight, and driven that all of this experience will become a blur to you. Enjoy the moment, not the end result. Everything you want to happen is going to happen.

There is a message from one of your future hit songs that I wish you could take in today: Notice some of the beauty around you. Partake in joy. And when you get the choice to watch on the sidelines or to dance, get out there and dance.

Love,
Lee Ann

TRISHA YEARWOOD

Singer and Songwriter

"Don't think your happiness depends on someone else."

RAISED IN MONTICELLO, Georgia, a town so tiny that it didn't even have a movie theater, Trisha Yearwood did the highly improbable: She carved out a phenomenal singing career. Her first, self-titled album went double platinum in 1992, and a single from it reached number one on the charts. She has since cut ten more albums—the eleventh, *Jasper County,* debuted in September of 2005—won two Grammy Awards, and performed at the Academy Awards, the Olympics' closing ceremonies, and the Library of Congress, among other venues.

Difficult as the music business is, establishing herself as a singer and songwriter seemed easier in many ways than defining herself as an individual. As a young woman, Trisha looked for validation from other people, she says. "It's something that a lot of us—especially women—do, and you spend a lot of years being somebody you're not because you're trying to please other people," she explains.

After her first decade in the music world she began to evaluate her life more carefully. "It's been incredible, but I made personal sacrifices to get there. So I've tried really hard for the last few years to really reconnect with the things that are important to me," she says. She's made a point of spending more time with her family—watching her sister's children play soccer, for example. The terror attacks on September 11 reinforced her choice. "They really got me focused. I'm grateful for the last ten years of my life, but I'd like the next ten years to be different. I'd like to make music, but I'd like to find a way to take what I do for a living and turn it into some way to help people," she explains.

Twice married and divorced, Trisha, now forty-two, is engaged to singer Garth Brooks. Here she writes to herself in her early twenties.

Dear Trisha,

I've got something to say to you, and I hope you will listen with an open heart. Don't be so worried about what everybody else thinks of you, and don't think your happiness depends on someone else. I want you to just trust yourself. Trust that if you take care of yourself on the inside, follow your instincts, and let yourself evolve naturally, your potential for happiness will be so much greater.

You probably don't think you need to hear this. Mama and Daddy brought you up to be independent, intelligent, and educated. And you are. I'm proud of the way you've stuck with your music, even though the odds were against you. But there's another part of you that's less independent. You're hearing everyone ask, "When are you going to get married?" The friends who didn't tie the knot right out of high school are doing it now, after college. Somewhere inside you, you think that's the way it's supposed to be.

There are going to be times when your gut instinct is telling you something isn't right, and you're going to go ahead with it anyway. If you keep that up, I know exactly what's going to happen: In about a year, you'll be standing in the back of a church with Daddy, getting ready to walk down the aisle. Daddy's going to say, jokingly, "We can duck out the back door if you want to." You won't dare tell him that's what you want to do.

Everybody will be sitting there, everything will have been paid for, and there will be a ton of cake to eat. You'll be afraid of the embarrassment of calling it off. And so you'll get married—for all the wrong reasons—to a wonderful guy.

There's another way of living, and it has brought me a sense of peace that I want you to have. Know that God has a plan for your life. Turn your life over to him every day. Stop looking outside yourself for validation and approval—you're letting other people define your happiness. Instead of trying so hard to manipulate life, take care of yourself on the inside. Then all those other attributes you're so desperately seeking will find you naturally.

Love,
Your forty-two-year-old
future self

PHOTO CREDITS

ABOUT THE AUTHOR

ELLYN SPRAGINS wrote the "Love & Money" column in the *New York Times* Sunday Business section for three years and is editor-at-large at *Fortune Small Business.* She has worked at Oxygen Media, *Newsweek, BusinessWeek, Smart Money,* and *Forbes,* and has written for *O, The Oprah Magazine; Working Woman;* and the *New York Times Magazine.* She lives in Pennington, New Jersey, with her husband and children.